HUMAN TRAFFICKING

A BIBLE STUDY ON AWARENESS AND PREVENTION

AMANDA C. MONTGOMERY

THE FOUNDRY PUBLISHING

Copyright © 2025 by Amanda C. Montgomery
The Foundry Publishing®
PO Box 419527
Kansas City, MO 64141
thefoundrypublishing.com

978-0-8341-4320-3

All rights reserved. No part of this publication may be reproduced, stored in a retrieval system, or transmitted in any form or by any means—for example, electronic, photocopy, recording—without the prior written permission of the publisher. The only exception is brief quotations in printed reviews.

Cover design: Caines Design
Interior design: Sharon Page

All Scripture quotations, unless indicated, are taken from THE HOLY BIBLE, NEW INTERNATIONAL VERSION®, NIV®. Copyright © 1973, 1978, 1984, 2011 by Biblica, Inc.® Used by permission. All rights reserved worldwide.

Scripture quotations marked (NLT) are from the *Holy Bible*, New Living Translation (NLT), copyright © 1996, 2004, 2015. Used by permission of Tyndale House Publishers, Inc., Wheaton, Illinois 60189. All rights reserved.

Scripture quotations marked (NRSVUE) are from the New Revised Standard Version, Updated Edition (NRSVUE). Copyright © 2021 National Council of Churches of Christ in the United States of America. Used by permission. All rights reserved worldwide.

Scripture quotations marked (CEB) are from the Common English Bible. Copyright © 2011 by the Common English Bible. All rights reserved. Used by permission.

Scripture quotations marked (RSV) are from the *Revised Standard Version* (RSV) of the Bible, copyright 1946, 1952, 1971 by the Division of Christian Education of the national Council of the Churches of Christ in the USA. Used by permission.

The internet addresses, email addresses, and phone numbers in this book are accurate at the time of publication. They are provided as a resource. The Foundry Publishing does not endorse them or vouch for their content or permanence.

CONTENTS

Introduction	5
Lesson 1: Standing Together in the Pain	**8**
Biblical Application of Lesson 1	18
Lesson 2: Betrayed by Someone You Know	**26**
Biblical Application of Lesson 2	34
Lesson 3: The God Who Sees	**46**
Biblical Application of Lesson 3	56
Lesson 4: "See if There Is Any Offensive Way in Me . . ."	**64**
Biblical Application of Lesson 4	79
Lesson 5: Vigilantes: Heroes or Villains?	**88**
Biblical Application of Lesson 5	100
Lesson 6: Sexual Assault against Men and Boys	**112**
Biblical Application of Lesson 6	121
Appendix A: Feeling Wheel	140
Appendix B: Trigger-Reducing Calming Techniques	141
Appendix C: Trafficking Awareness Resources for U.S. Residents	143

INTRODUCTION

Welcome! Thank you for embarking on this six-week journey to learn about sexual assault and exploitation in the Bible and how these important biblical accounts can help us better understand God's heart for victims, survivors, perpetrators, and the community in our broader world today.

Commercial sexual exploitation (CSE)—commonly referred to as "sex trafficking"—is a crime that hides in plain sight, and it is happening in our local communities. It thrives in the shadows by our lack of awareness, and it banks on our discomfort and preconceived notions. Research shows that teaching about the realities of CSE makes a significant impact.[1]

The purpose of this group is to discuss specifically how Christians should respond to the modern problem of CSE in light of the ancient examples we have in Scripture. Churches and Christian circles often find it difficult and uncomfortable to address sexual violence, so some Christians, even longtime believers, are surprised to discover how many accounts of sexual assault and exploitation there actually are in the Bible. Trauma is hard to talk about, but it happened in the Bible, and it still happens today. Scripture has great hope to share with all who have ears to hear. As we unpack what the Bible teaches about God's response to exploitation, we may conclude, as author and trauma expert Diane Langberg has suggested, that "trauma is perhaps the greatest mission field of the twenty-first century."[2]

---

1. See Amy Vatne Bintliff, Christine Stark, Lori DiPrete Brown, and Araceli Alonso, "Lifelong Wellbeing for Survivors of Sex Trafficking: Collaborative Perspectives from Survivors, Researchers, and Service Providers," *Dignity: A Journal on Sexual Exploitation and Violence* 3, no. 3 (October 2018). See also Nita Belles, *In Our Backyard: A Christian Perspective on Human Trafficking in the United States* (Nashville: Free River, 2011).
2. Diane Langberg, *Suffering and the Heart of God: How Trauma Destroys and Christ Restores* (Greensboro, NC: New Growth Press, 2015), 8.

Whether you are new to the Bible or have studied Scripture for years, this group is for you! Whether you are an expert in human trafficking prevention or you aren't sure you know anything other than what is portrayed in movies or in the news, you are in the right group! Regardless of your knowledge on the subject or the path that brought you here, thank you for your interest in learning and making a difference!

This study is arranged to focus on six group gatherings that will allow participants to learn stats, facts, and other relevant information about human trafficking; compare and apply modern trafficking realities with biblical scenarios; and discuss actions that anyone can take to recognize, interrupt, and prevent human trafficking in our own communities. Additional material will provide participants with opportunities to dig deeper between sessions, exploring a variety of biblical passages that illustrate God's reaction to oppressors and the oppressed. These chapters between sessions will help lay a biblical foundation to explore God's response to sexual assault and exploitation.

The study is designed to be utilized as a group study (but can also be used independently) by participants among the three populations that form the basic CSE system within any given community: CSE survivors, CSE perpetrators, and local community members. Although most groups who use the curriculum may identify as being from only one of these populations, all three groups will be addressed in order to offer each group a deeper understanding of how the CSE system works within the local context. Group discussion about CSE in the Bible and in a modern context may introduce participants to mild forms of trauma, potentially triggering those who have experienced primary or secondary trauma. Care has been taken to provide a curriculum that inspires participants to stay present in the midst of complex feelings, to allow Scripture to navigate a personal and communal healing process, and to motivate participants to embrace God-honoring and survivor-informed practices in the fight against trafficking.

Important note to anyone present who uses pornography, pays for, or profits from sexual exploitation: Thank you for your willingness and interest in participating in these next six weeks. Although little has been written about traffickers and sex buyers, the Bible has a lot to say. Sex-industry consumers have a particularly important role to play in ending sex trafficking. You will not be asked or expected in this group to identify your past or current sexual behaviors and consumer habits. However, as you commit to participating in this group for the next six weeks, please make a commitment to *yourself* (or to God) to abstain from pornography and sex buying of any kind for the duration of this study. Write down today's date to represent your first day of abstention from the kind of sexual behavior that harms yourself or others. Approach the content of this book with an open mind, and allow your assumptions to be challenged. At the end of the six weeks, you may find that you feel inclined toward a new perspective and lifestyle.

LESSON 1

Standing Together in the Pain

▪ Organizing Principle

Everyone has a role to play to prevent trafficking in the local community.

▪ Learning Objectives
- Identify the three groups that make up the basic system of commercial sexual exploitation (CSE) in the local community.
- Examine how local industries may profit from labor trafficking.
- Biblically investigate God's response to oppression, oppressor, and oppressed.

OPENING PRAYER

Ask someone to pray briefly for the group and for this session.

FEELINGS IDENTIFICATION

Each week, we'll begin by using the Feeling Wheel developed by Gloria Willcox (see Appendix A on page 140). Take a moment to examine the wheel and identify how you are currently feeling.

When you are ready, share one or two words from the wheel that represent how you are feeling right now. Do not explain the words you chose or comment on the words that others share.

The Feeling Wheel is a good tool to help us identify complex emotions, especially during difficult conversations. Please return to it as often as necessary during these group discussions when you would like help identifying or articulating feelings that arise.

LEARN TOGETHER

Thank you for choosing to embark on a study that dives into the tough topic of human trafficking. You may have mixed feelings or anxiety about this topic, and that's okay. The crime of human trafficking is dark and disturbing, but shedding light on the reality of this crime as it occurs locally is an important first step to reducing trafficking in our local communities. It's okay to acknowledge fear about this topic.

Here are some common initial sentiments that have been said by community members at the beginning of their learning journey.

Why should Christians learn about human trafficking? Sure, it's sad, but does it really have anything to do with me?

Does trafficking really happen in my town? How would I know?

This topic is so disturbing and literally discusses exploitative sex. Should we even be talking about it in church?

Do you resonate with any of these sentiments? Can you sense the tension of simultaneously wanting to learn while being afraid of what you might find out? If this is you, you are not alone. Utilizing the Feeling Wheel each week will help you embrace the transparency of mixed and complex feelings. People do not like to feel uncomfortable or out of control of their feelings, and exploring the topic of human trafficking can make us feel that way. In fact, trafficking tends to thrive in communities that don't know how to talk about it. Discussing human trafficking can feel daunting, but you are already making a difference by choosing to learn.

There are three main groups that make up the basic system of human trafficking in local communities, and each of us fits into one or more of these groups. The three main groups are:

1) Victims and Survivors: Anyone who has been exploited for sex or labor

2) Perpetrators: Anyone who has paid for or profited from sex or labor trafficking

3) Local Community: Everyone who lives or works in a local community

It is important to keep all three groups in mind when learning about human trafficking. One common detriment to conversations about human trafficking is that it tends to focus on one group while ignoring the presence and actions of the other two groups. The most common mistake is to focus on the plight of victims and survivors without acknowledging the reality that perpetrators exist in the same community. Discussing the presence of all three groups enables us to recognize whether a community context is ignoring or acknowledging the crime of trafficking and acting on this information accordingly.

Another important reason to acknowledge the presence of all three groups is hope. Each participant, regardless of their path, can become an anti-trafficking advocate. As you may already know, many trafficking survivors have led the charge in local, national, and international platforms to create better definitions, policies, and laws to reduce exploitation.

Perpetrators can also play an important role in ending human trafficking. Former sex buyers can help shed light on portions of the crime that often go unrecognized. It is estimated that there are roughly 40 to 180 sex buyers to every 1 person being sex-trafficked.[1] Ending this pattern and creating space for perpetrator accountability groups could be a crucial step forward. Additionally, ex-traffickers have been known to help in the anti-trafficking effort by shedding light on the innerworkings of the crime. There are a few former traffickers who now work in the anti-trafficking field.

The largest group—the local community—has the potential to play a vital role. Community members are the eyes, ears, hands, and feet of the local community. The community must learn to recognize and respond appropriately. Without community

---

1. Rachel Moran, *Paid For: My Journey through Prostitution* (New York: W. W. Norton & Company, 2015), 192–94.

engagement, red flags won't be noticed, resources can't be provided, and anti-trafficking policies are unable to be passed.

Each of these three groups has the potential to be part of the solution. Christians in particular should be compelled to learn about trafficking prevention and awareness because bringing people out of the darkness and into the light is the very work of the Holy Spirit, and we are called to engage in this work—starting with ourselves.

Scripture and Discussion

One of the most popular, well-known verses in the Bible is **John 3:16**:

For God so loved the world that he gave his one and only Son, that whoever believes in him shall not perish but have eternal life.

Then **verse 17** gives us a less well-known but really important follow-up:

For God did not send his Son into the world to condemn the world, but to save the world through him.

This is good news for all of us! Some may think, *If God only knew . . .*

More good news! God does already know. The Lord knows what each of us has been through, so there is no need to hide from a God who sees. Our loving God has provided a pathway out of the darkness and into the light.

Read **John 3:19–21** together:

[19]This is the verdict: Light has come into the world, but people loved darkness instead of light because their deeds were evil. [20]Everyone who does evil hates the light, and will not come into the light for fear that their deeds will be exposed. [21]But whoever lives by the truth comes into the light, so that it may be seen plainly that what they have done has been done in the sight of God.

1. What do you think it means in verse 19 when it says light has come into the world?

2. Why do evil deeds correspond with loving darkness?

3. What is the relationship between truth and light in this passage?

4. What does it mean to live by the truth?

_____
_____
_____
_____
_____

Trafficking and Discussion

Just as the scripture from John says about evil deeds loving darkness, human trafficking also thrives in the dark shadows and blind spots of our communities. Communities that ignore their own blind spots provide places for CSE to thrive under the radar. Using Scripture as our guide, we will shine light into the darkness within ourselves and our communities. As we peel back the layers of sexual exploitation in the Bible and in our modern-day communities, you may discover dark shadows you had not previously recognized in yourself or in your community. Remember that God knew before you did. Bring it before the Lord and come into the light. We can learn to live by the truth and come into the light in all aspects of our lives. This is good news!

So what *is* human trafficking? Human trafficking is a crime that involves exploiting a person for labor, services, or commercial sex. Let's look at the legal definition. It may be helpful to read it out loud to the group:

In the United States, the Trafficking Victims Protection Act of 2000, and its subsequent reauthorizations, define human trafficking as:
   a) *Sex trafficking in which a commercial sex act is induced by force, fraud, or coercion, or in which the person induced to perform such act has not attained 18 years of age; or*
   b) *The recruitment, harboring, transportation, provision, or obtaining of a person for labor or services, through the use of force, fraud, or coercion for the purpose of subjection to involuntary servitude, peonage, debt bondage, or slavery.*[2]

---

2. The United States Department of Justice, "Human Trafficking," https://www.justice.gov/humantrafficking.

The term "commercial sex act" means any sex act (stripping, physical or digital pornography, dancing, sexting, physical intercourse, etc.) on account of which anything of value (food, shelter, clothing, money, drugs, or the promise of safety) is given to or received by any person.

Notice in the legal definition that force, fraud, or coercion need not be present for a minor to be trafficked.

1. Why do you think this may be the case?

_____

_____

_____

_____

_____

_____

2. How might this definition change a community's understanding about sexually exploited teens?

_____

_____

_____

_____

_____

_____

Human trafficking is one of the most profitable crimes in the world, second only to drug trafficking.[3] If current trends continue, human trafficking is projected to eventually surpass drug trafficking in terms of profitability.

---

3. Attorney General of Washington, "Human Trafficking," Washington State Office of the Attorney General, 2019, https://www.atg.wa.gov/human-trafficking.

There are three main reasons that trafficking people might be more lucrative than trafficking drugs:

1) Force, fraud, and coercion
A victim can be manipulated to say that their own exploitation is voluntary. They may say it out of fear of harm to self or loved ones, or they may say it out of loyalty to the person harming them. **A minor cannot give consent.** Any commercial sex act involving a minor is sex trafficking.[4]

2) Anonymity and lower penalties
There is a higher chance of getting caught trafficking drugs than trafficking people, and penalties tend to be more severe for drug traffickers.[5] It is also harder to locate a human trafficker because they do not need to be at the location where trafficking occurs in order to make a profit. Often the victims, rather than the traffickers, are arrested.

3) Product
Drugs are sold and then consumed, but people can be sold over and over again. Online pornography can be distributed for profit without limit—even if the victim has escaped or died.[6] Often perpetrators use pornographic images to blackmail victims, threatening to publicly expose them if they ever try to retaliate.

It is important to note that there are two main categories of human trafficking:
1) Labor Trafficking
2) Sex Trafficking

This study focuses primarily on sex trafficking, but labor trafficking is also prominent in the Bible and in local communities. In most communities, more research, funds, and resources have been devoted to sex-trafficking prevention than labor-trafficking prevention.

---

4. 106th Congress, "Victims of Trafficking and Violence Protection Act of 2000," Public Law 106–386 (2000), Section 1002.
5. Attorney General of Washington, "Human Trafficking."
6. "I Am Jane Doe," Online Video, *I Am Jane Doe Film* (50 Eggs Films, November 18, 2016), https://www.iamjanedoefilm.com.

Industries that have been known to exploit people for labor[7] include but are not limited to:

- Healthcare/Home Health
- Trucking
- Janitorial/House Cleaning
- Construction
- Manufacturing
- Agriculture/Farming
- Hospitality/Hotels/Food Service
- Nannies
- Forestry/Logging
- Sales/Traveling Sales
- Landscaping
- Nail Salons/Hair Salons

As a group, choose an industry from this list that is present in your community and discuss the following questions:

1. How might labor trafficking happen in that industry? Use the legal definition of trafficking to consider how the crime could occur.

2. What are some obstacles that keep the community from recognizing this form of trafficking?

---

7. Polaris, "The Typology of Modern Slavery," October 16, 2019, https://polarisproject.org/the-typology-of-modern-slavery/.

3. What questions would you want to ask of your own community to discover the obstacles around recognizing and ending trafficking in this industry?

CLOSING

Today we have begun our six-week journey. We have discussed the three main groups that make up the system of CSE, and we have learned that all three groups have the potential to become allies in the fight against trafficking. We have read the legal definition of human trafficking and recognize that it can take many forms. At times, sex trafficking and labor trafficking can be independent of each other; other times, they overlap, adding layers to the trauma of those being exploited.

The labor-trafficking list is not meant to be exhaustive. It is meant to help the community better recognize where human trafficking might occur. In the next few weeks, we will explore how trafficking occurs, red flags to look for, and resources for what to do if you suspect human trafficking is happening in your community.

Close your time together by praying **Psalm 10:17–18** (NLT): *Lord, you know the hopes of the helpless. Surely you will hear their cries and comfort them. You will bring justice to the orphans and the oppressed, so mere people can no longer terrify them.*

Biblical Application of Lesson 1
DAY 1

This week, we began by discussing Jesus's most famous words in John 3:16 and continued through John 3:21.

1. In this passage in John 3, what does Jesus say that God loves, and what does Jesus say that people love?

   _____
   _____
   _____
   _____
   _____
   _____

2. How are these desires opposed?

   _____
   _____
   _____
   _____
   _____
   _____

3. How do these verses differentiate those who come into the light from those who stay in the darkness?

_____

_____

_____

_____

_____

_____

_____

_____

_____

4. Whose truth matters when it comes to the differentiation of darkness and light?

_____

_____

_____

_____

_____

_____

_____

_____

_____

Biblical Application of Lesson 1
DAY 2

At the beginning of Jesus's public ministry, he went to the synagogue in his hometown of Nazareth and read the scroll of the prophet Isaiah.

Read **Luke 4:16–21**:

[16]He went to Nazareth. where he had been brought up, and on the Sabbath day he went into the synagogue, as was his custom. He stood up to read, [17]and the scroll of the prophet Isaiah was handed to him. Unrolling it, he found the place where it is written:

[18]"The Spirit of the Lord is on me,
because he has anointed me to proclaim good news to the poor.
He has sent me to proclaim freedom for the prisoners
and recovery of sight for the blind,
to set the oppressed free,
[19]to proclaim the year of the Lord's favor."

[20]Then he rolled up the scroll, gave it back to the attendant and sat down. The eyes of everyone in the synagogue were fastened on him. [21]He began by saying to them, "Today this scripture is fulfilled in your hearing."

1. God is both loving and just. What does God care about? What does God see?

2. What are some practical ways that Christians are being called to live by the truth and come into the light?

_____

_____

_____

_____

_____

_____

_____

_____

_____

3. God's people are called to love what God loves and respond accordingly, but what happens when God's people harm others? How might God respond when God's people are the abusers?

_____

_____

_____

_____

_____

_____

_____

Biblical Application of Lesson 1
DAY 3

Read Ezekiel 34.

1. This chapter indicates that God's people can be both the oppressors *and* the victims. We who follow God are called to be good shepherds, but what happens when God's people devour the sheep rather than protecting them?

   _____
   _____
   _____
   _____

2. How might this chapter enrich your understanding of God as the Good Shepherd?

   _____
   _____
   _____
   _____

3. How are Christians called to be good shepherds?

   _____
   _____
   _____
   _____

Biblical Application of Lesson 1
DAY 4

1. Refer to **Luke 4:18–19** and consider more ways that Christians are called to be good shepherds.

   _____

   _____

   _____

   _____

2. Think back on the group discussion about how sex and labor trafficking can thrive in the shadows of the local community. Imagine yourself as a shepherd and the local community as your pastureland. Referring to what you have learned from Ezekiel 34 and Luke 4:18–19, how might you view your local community differently from this perspective?

   _____

   _____

   _____

   _____

3. Think from the perspective of a community member. What questions should community members be asking to uncover their own shortcomings and the shortcomings of the larger community in relation to human trafficking?

   _____

   _____

   _____

   _____

4. Think from the perspective of a survivor. What might a survivor wish the local community understood about trafficking? What might survivors wish the community understood about them?

_____

_____

_____

_____

_____

_____

5. Think from the perspective of a perpetrator. What might deter a perpetrator from exploiting someone in the future? What might be a situation where a perpetrator or former perpetrator might choose to protect someone instead of exploiting them?

_____

_____

_____

_____

_____

6. How can trafficking be reduced in the local community?

_____

_____

_____

_____

_____

_____

7. Write a prayer for your local community.

LESSON 2

Betrayed by Someone You Know

■ Organizing Principle

Biblical accounts of sexual assault record God's response to victims, perpetrators, and the community.

■ Learning Objectives
- Classify CSE as a more specific form of the broader crime of sexual assault.
- Apply the legal definition of human trafficking to biblical and modern-day trafficking accounts.
- Discuss variables that cause trafficking to thrive in the modern-day context.

OPENING PRAYER

Ask someone to pray briefly for the group and for this session.

FEELINGS IDENTIFICATION

Locate the Feeling Wheel at the back of the book (page 140). Take a moment to examine the wheel and identify how you are currently feeling.

When you are ready, share one or two words from the wheel that represent how you are feeling right now. Do not explain the words you chose or comment on the words that others share.

DEBRIEF THE WEEK

Share with one another what you have been processing since the last meeting, considering prior discussion and any engagement you did with the mid-week biblical application lessons. Trauma-related content can be difficult to process and discuss. This time is meant to give participants a chance to process recent content before introducing this week's topic.

LEARN TOGETHER

Research indicates that one in four women and one in six men have been sexually assaulted.[1] That's a lot of people!

If this is your story, you are not alone. The Bible has much to say about sexual assault. Although this study is designed to help Christians gain awareness of how commercial sexual exploitation happens in the local community, it is important to note that CSE is a specific type of crime that fits under the broader umbrella of sexual assault. The same scripture that will be used to open our knowledge about CSE is also a scripture that discusses sexual assault in general.

If you are among those who have been sexually assaulted, or if you know someone who has been sexually assaulted, allow these scriptures to speak to you and your healing journey.

Today we will read two biblical accounts of sexual exploitation that occurred within the most prominent family in the Bible. We will allow these scriptures to guide our discussion as we consider the actions of the people involved as well as God's response. These stories may be difficult to read. Remember that the purpose of studying Scripture is to learn and cultivate God's character in our relationship with God and with others.

---

1. 1 in 6, "The 1 in 6 Statistic," https://1in6.org/statistic/.

Scripture and Discussion

Read **Genesis 12:10–20** together:

¹⁰*Now there was a famine in the land, and Abram went down to Egypt to live there for a while because the famine was severe.* ¹¹*As he was about to enter Egypt, he said to his wife Sarai, "I know what a beautiful woman you are.* ¹²*When the Egyptians see you, they will say, 'This is his wife.' Then they will kill me but will let you live.* ¹³*Say you are my sister, so that I will be treated well for your sake and my life will be spared because of you."*

¹⁴*When Abram came to Egypt, the Egyptians saw that Sarai was a very beautiful woman.* ¹⁵*And when Pharaoh's officials saw her, they praised her to Pharaoh, and she was taken into his palace.* ¹⁶*He treated Abram well for her sake, and Abram acquired sheep and cattle, male and female donkeys, male and female servants, and camels.*

¹⁷*But the L*ORD *inflicted serious diseases on Pharaoh and his household because of Abram's wife Sarai.* ¹⁸*So Pharaoh summoned Abram. "What have you done to me?" he said. "Why didn't you tell me she was your wife?* ¹⁹*Why did you say, 'She is my sister,' so that I took her to be my wife? Now then, here is your wife. Take her and go!"* ²⁰*Then Pharaoh gave orders about Abram to his men, and they sent him on his way, with his wife and everything he had.*

Read **Genesis 20** together:

¹*Now Abraham moved on from there into the region of the Negev and lived between Kadesh and Shur. For a while he stayed in Gerar,* ²*and there Abraham said of his wife Sarah, "She is my sister." Then Abimelek king of Gerar sent for Sarah and took her.*

³*But God came to Abimelek in a dream one night and said to him, "You are as good as dead because of the woman you have taken; she is a married woman."*

⁴*Now Abimelek had not gone near her, so he said, "Lord, will you destroy an innocent nation?* ⁵*Did he not say to me, 'She is my sister,' and didn't she also say, 'He is my brother'? I have done this with a clear conscience and clean hands."*

⁶*Then God said to him in the dream, "Yes, I know you did this with a clear conscience, and so I have kept you from sinning against me. That is why I did not let you touch her.* ⁷*Now return the man's wife, for he is a prophet, and he will pray for you*

and you will live. But if you do not return her, you may be sure that you and all who belong to you will die."

⁸Early the next morning Abimelek summoned all his officials, and when he told them all that had happened, they were very much afraid. ⁹Then Abimelek called Abraham in and said, "What have you done to us? How have I wronged you that you have brought such great guilt upon me and my kingdom? You have done things to me that should never be done." ¹⁰And Abimelek asked Abraham, "What was your reason for doing this?"

¹¹Abraham replied, "I said to myself, 'There is surely no fear of God in this place, and they will kill me because of my wife.' ¹²Besides, she really is my sister, the daughter of my father though not of my mother; and she became my wife. ¹³And when God had me wander from my father's household, I said to her, 'This is how you can show your love to me: Everywhere we go, say of me, "He is my brother."'"

¹⁴Then Abimelek brought sheep and cattle and male and female slaves and gave them to Abraham, and he returned Sarah his wife to him. ¹⁵And Abimelek said, "My land is before you; live wherever you like."

¹⁶To Sarah he said, "I am giving your brother a thousand shekels of silver. This is to cover the offense against you before all who are with you; you are completely vindicated."

¹⁷Then Abraham prayed to God, and God healed Abimelek, his wife and his female slaves so they could have children again, ¹⁸for the Lord had kept all the women in Abimelek's household from conceiving because of Abraham's wife Sarah.

1. Why was Abraham afraid on these two occasions?

_____

_____

_____

_____

_____

2. What actions did Abraham take to protect himself?

_____
_____
_____
_____
_____
_____
_____

3. What actions did Abraham take to protect his wife?

_____
_____
_____
_____
_____
_____
_____

4. Who rescued Sarah, and how?

_____
_____
_____
_____
_____

5. What wealth did Abraham receive from Pharaoh in exchange for Sarah (Genesis 12)?

6. What wealth did Abraham receive from Abimelek in the end (Genesis 20)?

7. Hagar—who eventually became the mother of Abraham's first son and was subsequently treated unfairly by both Abraham and Sarah—was an Egyptian slave in Abraham and Sarah's household. What do you think might be Hagar's connection to the story in Genesis 12?

Trafficking and Discussion

As a reminder, the legal definition of human trafficking in the United States is:

a) *Sex trafficking in which a commercial sex act is induced by force, fraud, or coercion, or in which the person induced to perform such act has not attained 18 years of age; or*

b) *The recruitment, harboring, transportation, provision, or obtaining of a person for labor or services, through the use of force, fraud, or coercion for the purpose of subjection to involuntary servitude, peonage, debt bondage, or slavery.*

Going by this definition, Abraham trafficked Sarah twice. He received great wealth by receiving Pharaoh's extravagant gifts in exchange for Sarah. It was common for kings to have a household full of multiple wives and concubines. Without God's intervention, there was no reason to assume Sarah would ever have been released from Pharaoh or Abimelek.

It may feel jarring to hear Abraham's actions toward Sarah in these scriptures called "human trafficking." Use the Feeling Wheel to identify how you are feeling right now. Take turns sharing the word that describes how you feel for Abraham's actions to be described as trafficking. You do not have to explain why you feel that way; simply share the word or words.

Research estimates that 80 percent of adults and 93 percent of children who are sexually assaulted knew the perpetrator prior to the abuse.[2] Similarly, the majority of CSE survivors are initially trafficked by someone they know.[3]

Survivors of both sexual assault and CSE have expressed that they experienced great distress, shock, denial, and feelings of betrayal when someone they knew, trusted, or loved hurt them.

Given these statistics, consider how unhelpful awareness training like "stranger danger" could be for minors.

---

2. RAINN, "Children and Teens: Statistics," https://www.rainn.org/statistics/children-and-teens.
3. Polaris, "Child Sex Trafficking," https://polarisproject.org/child-sex-trafficking/.

1. How might "stranger danger" training fail to prepare children to recognize safety issues when the perpetrator is someone they already know and have previously trusted?

_____

_____

_____

_____

2. What might be other age-appropriate ways to make kids aware of dangerous people and learn how to seek help? (Consider how we can talk to kids about actions, about recognizing red flags, and about adults they trust asking them to keep secrets, etc.)

_____

_____

_____

_____

CLOSING

Take a moment right now to be silent and think about how you are feeling. Let these feelings inspire you to pray silently for those who are being harmed by someone they know. Use the pain you may be feeling in this moment to lift before the Lord those who are suffering from past or present betrayals.

Thankfully, God rescued Sarah twice. But what about the victims who are never rescued? Next week, we will explore the biblical account of two women who were forced to spend their entire lives in bondage. We will learn about God's compassion for them and find out why it is important to tell their story.

Close your time together by praying **Psalm 116:1–2**: *I love the* Lord, *for he heard my voice; he heard my cry for mercy. Because he turned his ear to me, I will call on him as long as I live.*

Biblical Application of Lesson 2

DAY 1

As you read the two Genesis accounts during your lesson 2 session, did you notice that Abraham and Sarah's names changed between accounts? In Genesis 12, they were still Abram and Sarai. God had already asked Abram to go to the land God had promised (see Genesis 12:1), but God had not yet established a covenant with Abram promising him descendants as numerous as the stars (see Genesis 15), nor had God yet changed Abram and Sarai's names to Abraham and Sarah (see Genesis 17). Both of these things happened after the Pharaoh encounter in Genesis 12 but before the Abimelek encounter in Genesis 20.

Read **Genesis 16:1–6**, another story that occurs between the Pharaoh and Abimelek accounts. God has now made the covenant with Abram to increase his descendants, but we see that Abram and Sarai have grown impatient with God's timing and have attempted to fulfill God's promise by forcing their slave Hagar to be impregnated by Abram:

¹*Now Sarai, Abram's wife, had borne him no children. But she had an Egyptian slave named Hagar;* ²*so she said to Abram, "The Lord has kept me from having children. Go, sleep with my slave; perhaps I can build a family through her."*

Abram agreed to what Sarai said. ³*So after Abram had been living in Canaan ten years, Sarai his wife took her Egyptian slave Hagar and gave her to her husband to be his wife.* ⁴*He slept with Hagar, and she conceived.*

When she knew she was pregnant, she began to despise her mistress. ⁵*Then Sarai said to Abram, "You are responsible for the wrong I am suffering. I put my slave in your arms, and now that she knows she is pregnant, she despises me. May the Lord judge between you and me."*

⁶*"Your slave is in your hands," Abram said. "Do with her whatever you think best." Then Sarai mistreated Hagar; so she fled from her.*

1. Whom did Sarai think should receive rights to the birth of a child between Abram and Hagar (see v. 2)?

2. Who was looking out for Hagar's safety and dignity in this story?

3. What do these verses tell us about Sarai and Abram?

4. Hagar, pregnant and mistreated, decides it would be better to flee to the desert than stay in Abram and Sarai's household. Using the Feeling Wheel, list some of the emotions Hagar must have felt.

_____

_____

_____

_____

_____

Biblical Application of Lesson 2
DAY 2

Read **Genesis 16:7–15**:

⁷The angel of the Lord found Hagar near a spring in the desert; it was the spring that is beside the road to Shur. ⁸And he said, "Hagar, slave of Sarai, where have you come from, and where are you going?"

"I'm running away from my mistress Sarai," she answered.

⁹Then the angel of the Lord told her, "Go back to your mistress and submit to her." ¹⁰The angel added, "I will increase your descendants so much that they will be too numerous to count."

¹¹The angel of the Lord also said to her:

"You are now pregnant
and you will give birth to a son.
You shall name him Ishmael,
for the Lord has heard of your misery.
¹²He will be a wild donkey of a man;
his hand will be against everyone
and everyone's hand against him,
and he will live in hostility
toward all his brothers."

¹³She gave this name to the Lord who spoke to her: "You are the God who sees me," for she said, "I have now seen the One who sees me." ¹⁴That is why the well was called Beer Lahai Roi; it is still there, between Kadesh and Bered.

¹⁵So Hagar bore Abram a son, and Abram gave the name Ishmael to the son she had borne.

Hagar receives a blessing in **verse 10**. Compare this blessing to the blessing God gave Abram in **Genesis 15:5**: *He took him outside and said, "Look up at the sky and count the stars—if indeed you can count them." Then he said to him, "So shall your offspring be."*

1. What are the similarities and differences between these two blessings??

   _____
   _____
   _____
   _____
   _____
   _____
   _____

2. The angel of the Lord spoke over Hagar's unborn son (**vv. 9–12**). These verses have been compared to **Luke 1:26–33**, when the angel Gabriel announced to Mary that she would bear a son. Read the Luke passage and note some of the similarities and differences between these messages. How did each woman respond?

   _____
   _____
   _____
   _____
   _____
   _____
   _____

3. Hagar is the first person recorded in the Bible to give God a name. She calls him "the God who sees me" (v. 13). Write a prayer of thanksgiving to the God who sees.

_____

_____

_____

_____

_____

_____

_____

4. If God is compassionate, why might God have commanded Hagar to return to Abram and Sarai's household?

_____

_____

_____

_____

_____

_____

_____

Read **Genesis 17:18–27** to discover God's blessing and confirmation for Ishmael and his descendants.

Biblical Application of Lesson 2
DAY 3

By the time Abraham and Sarah encountered King Abimelek, God had already changed Abraham and Sarah's names, Ishmael had been born, blessed, and circumcised into the covenant under Abraham, and Isaac had already been promised by God to be conceived by Sarah.

Read Genesis 20:1–3:

1Now Abraham moved on from there into the region of the Negev and lived between Kadesh and Shur. For a while he stayed in Gerar, 2and there Abraham said of his wife Sarah, "She is my sister." Then Abimelek king of Gerar sent for Sarah and took her.

3But God came to Abimelek in a dream one night and said to him, "You are as good as dead because of the woman you have taken; she is a married woman."

1. When Sarah was taken into King Abimelek's household, who remained in Abraham's household?

2. Using the Feeling Wheel, identify some words that you think describe how Sarah might have felt as she returned home.

_____

_____

_____

_____

_____

_____

_____

After Sarah returned, she conceived and gave birth to the son God had promised her—Isaac (see Genesis 21). After Isaac's birth, Sarah's violence toward Hagar continued. Even though Sarah played an instrumental role in bringing about Ishmael's birth, her perspective changed drastically. Compare Sarah's words in **Genesis 16:2** to her words in **Genesis 21:10**.

Sarah sent Hagar and Ishmael into the wilderness to die. **Read Genesis 21:8–20**:

⁸*The child grew and was weaned, and on the day Isaac was weaned Abraham held a great feast.* ⁹*But Sarah saw that the son whom Hagar the Egyptian had borne to Abraham was mocking,* ¹⁰*and she said to Abraham, "Get rid of that slave woman and her son, for that woman's son will never share in the inheritance with my son Isaac."*

¹¹*The matter distressed Abraham greatly because it concerned his son.* ¹²*But God said to him, "Do not be so distressed about the boy and your slave woman. Listen to whatever Sarah tells you, because it is through Isaac that your offspring will be reckoned.* ¹³*I will make the son of the slave into a nation also, because he is your offspring."*

¹⁴*Early the next morning Abraham took some food and a skin of water and gave them to Hagar. He set them on her shoulders and then sent her off with the boy. She went on her way and wandered in the Desert of Beersheba.*

¹⁵When the water in the skin was gone, she put the boy under one of the bushes. ¹⁶Then she went off and sat down about a bowshot away, for she thought, "I cannot watch the boy die." And as she sat there, she began to sob.

¹⁷God heard the boy crying, and the angel of God called to Hagar from heaven and said to her, "What is the matter, Hagar? Do not be afraid; God has heard the boy crying as he lies there. ¹⁸Lift the boy up and take him by the hand, for I will make him into a great nation."

¹⁹Then God opened her eyes and she saw a well of water. So she went and filled the skin with water and gave the boy a drink.

²⁰God was with the boy as he grew up. He lived in the desert and became an archer.

3. How did God respond to Hagar?

_____

_____

_____

_____

_____

_____

4. How long did God stay with Ishmael?

_____

_____

_____

_____

_____

_____

5. Something that can be difficult to come to terms with when reading these stories in Genesis is the reality that Sarah was both a victim and a perpetrator of human trafficking. In Genesis 20 and 21, we see Sarah both being abused herself and choosing to abuse others. Why might she have perpetuated another woman's abuse after her own experiences? Use the Feeling Wheel to speculate about Sarah's emotions in these stories.

_____

_____

_____

_____

_____

_____

_____

_____

Biblical Application of Lesson 2
DAY 4

1. What was new for you in the Genesis stories you read and studied this week?

   _____
   _____
   _____
   _____
   _____
   _____
   _____
   _____

2. Whom do you view the most compassionately, and why?

   _____
   _____
   _____
   _____
   _____
   _____
   _____

3. Name one way that God showed compassion amid suffering in these stories.

___

4. Sarah and Hagar were both released from bondage, but their wounds ran deep. Write a prayer for those who are healing from the aftereffects of sexual assault and human trafficking.

___

LESSON 3

The God Who Sees

■ Organizing Principle

Sex trafficking victims and perpetrators are hidden in plain sight in the Bible and in the local community.

■ Learning Objectives

- Discuss moments in Scripture when God's response diverges from human intentions or expectations.
- Construct phrases that challenge community opinions about victims and perpetrators of CSE.
- Recognize common CSE red flags and recommended anti-trafficking responses.

OPENING PRAYER

Ask someone to pray briefly for the group and for this session.

FEELINGS IDENTIFICATION

Locate the Feeling Wheel at the back of the book (page 140). Take a moment to examine the wheel and identify how you are currently feeling.

When you are ready, share one or two words from the wheel that represent how you are feeling right now. Do not explain the words you chose or comment on the words that others share.

DEBRIEF THE WEEK

Share with one another what you have been processing since the last meeting, considering prior discussion and any engagement you did with the mid-week biblical application lessons. Trauma-related content can be difficult to process and discuss. This time is meant to give participants a chance to process recent content before introducing this week's topic.

LEARN TOGETHER

Human trafficking thrives in the shadows. In both the Old and New Testaments, the Bible likens sin to darkness, explaining that the remedy is to come into the light. Jesus says in John 3:19–21, *"This is the verdict: Light has come into the world, but people loved darkness instead of light because their deeds were evil. Everyone who does evil hates the light, and will not come into the light for fear that their deeds will be exposed. But whoever lives by the truth comes into the light, so that it may be seen plainly that what they have done has been done in the sight of God."*

Today we will observe how God shines a light on the dark shadows lurking within a popular account in the Old Testament. Most of the time, this story is told in a way that highlights two sisters without ever recognizing the abuse within the household. Those who grew up in the church may be familiar with Jacob's wives, Rachel and Leah. Now it's time to get to know Bilhah and Zilpah.

Abraham's grandson Jacob married two sisters named Leah and Rachel. As a wedding gift, their father, Laban, gave each daughter a maidservant from his household. Leah acquired Zilpah as a servant, and Rachel acquired Bilhah. Scripture records that Jacob favored Rachel more than Leah even though Leah was the first of his wives to have children. The two sisters competed to provide heirs for Jacob. Leah bore four sons in her attempts to win Jacob's love. Rachel, for the time being, remained childless (see Genesis 29:31–35).

Scripture and Discussion
Read **Genesis 30:1–13** together:

¹When Rachel saw that she wasn't having any children for Jacob, she became jealous of her sister. She pleaded with Jacob, "Give me children, or I'll die!"

²*Then Jacob became furious with Rachel. "Am I God?" he asked. "He's the one who has kept you from having children!"*

³*Then Rachel told him, "Take my maid, Bilhah, and sleep with her. She will bear children for me, and through her I can have a family, too." ⁴So Rachel gave her servant, Bilhah, to Jacob as a wife, and he slept with her. ⁵Bilhah became pregnant and presented him with a son. ⁶Rachel named him Dan, for she said, "God has vindicated me! He has heard my request and given me a son." ⁷Then Bilhah became pregnant again and gave Jacob a second son. ⁸Rachel named him Naphtali, for she said, "I have struggled hard with my sister, and I'm winning!"*

⁹*Meanwhile, Leah realized that she wasn't getting pregnant anymore, so she took her servant, Zilpah, and gave her to Jacob as a wife. ¹⁰Soon Zilpah presented him with a son. ¹¹Leah named him Gad, for she said, "How fortunate I am!" ¹²Then Zilpah gave Jacob a second son. And Leah named him Asher, for she said, "What joy is mine! Now the other women will celebrate with me." (NLT)*

1. Whom did Rachel believe should receive credit for Bilhah's children?

_____

_____

_____

_____

2. The very meaning of each son's name told a story. Rachel named Bilhah's sons Dan and Naphtali. What did these names mean? (Hint: use a Bible to look at the footnotes.)

_____

_____

_____

_____

3. Even though she already had four biological sons, Leah forced Zilpah to have children on her behalf. Leah named Zilpah's sons Gad and Asher. What did these names mean?

_____

_____

_____

_____

4. Altogether, Bilhah and Zilpah bore four of the twelve sons who became leaders of the twelve tribes of Israel. The names of these two women were recorded and preserved in Scripture. Who in our modern-day context might be encouraged by reading Bilhah and Zilpah's names in the Bible, and why?

_____

_____

_____

_____

_____

Read **Genesis 35:22b–26** together:
Jacob had twelve sons:

[23]*The sons of Leah:*
Reuben the firstborn of Jacob, Simeon, Levi, Judah, Issachar and Zebulun.

[24]*The sons of Rachel:*
Joseph and Benjamin.

[25]*The sons of Rachel's servant Bilhah:*
Dan and Naphtali.

²⁶*The sons of Leah's servant Zilpah:*
Gad and Asher.

These were the sons of Jacob, who were born to him in Paddan Aram.

1. What stands out to you about the order in which these sons are listed?

_____

_____

_____

_____

2. Regardless of Rachel and Leah's attempts to lay claim to these children, what does the Bible indicate?

_____

_____

_____

_____

Read Genesis 49:16–21 together:
¹⁶*Dan will provide justice for his people*
as one of the tribes of Israel.
¹⁷*Dan will be a snake by the roadside,*
a viper along the path,
that bites the horse's heels
so that its rider tumbles backward.

¹⁸*I look for your deliverance, L*ORD.

¹⁹*Gad will be attacked by a band of raiders,*
but he will attack them at their heels.

²⁰*Asher's food will be rich;*
he will provide delicacies fit for a king.

²¹*Naphtali is a doe set free*
that bears beautiful fawns.

1. These verses are Jacob's blessings over his sons. Look back at what Rachel and Leah named these four sons of Bilhah and Zilpah. How are their father's blessings over them related to the meanings of their names?

_____

_____

_____

_____

_____

Trafficking and Discussion

Many CSE victims and perpetrators hide in plain sight. Why do communities have a hard time recognizing victims and perpetrators?

1) It's easy to deny abuse.
- State a phrase that represents denial that Zilpah and Bilhah are being abused.
- State a phrase that shines light on their abuse by eliminating denial.

2) It's easy to justify the perpetrator's actions.
- State a phrase that justifies Jacob's, Rachel's, or Leah's actions toward Zilpah and Bilhah.
- State a phrase that shines light on their abuse by eliminating the justification of sinful actions.

3) It's easy to blame the victim.
- State one phrase that blames Zilpah and Bilhah for the abuse that has happened to them.
- State a phrase that shines light on the abuse by holding the perpetrator accountable.

When darkness is left unchecked, a community is primed to protect perpetrators and blame victims. In a community that denies its own shadows, CSE victims and survivors do not know whom they can trust.

1. Whom, if anyone, could Zilpah and Bilhah have turned to in the family or community to end their abuse?

_____

_____

_____

_____

2. How might your church or local community be protecting shadows and darkness without even knowing it? (Consider what Zilpah and Bilhah needed and come up with ways that the church can become a safer space for people who need help.)

_____

_____

_____

_____

3. How could your church or local community work to earn the trust of survivors or others in the community who need someone to turn to? (Consider ideas that emphasize treating survivors with compassion and dignity.)

_____

_____

_____

_____

Many people victimized by sex trafficking never get out. Today, the average lifespan for someone who is being sex trafficked is thirty-four years. Often, the cause of death is homicide by buyer or trafficker.[1]

It is not enough for the community to feel sympathy for the plight of trafficking victims. The community must feel a sense of responsibility for the shadows it produces through denial, justification, and blame. If we learn to see what is happening in the community, then we can understand how to recognize red flags and respond accordingly.

Here is a list of red flags indicating that a person is potentially being labor- or sex-trafficked in the local community:[2]

Minors
- Multiple texting apps
- Multiple accounts on the same social media platform
- Dating adults
- Second phone or expensive new phone not paid for by caregivers
- In possession of sexual paraphernalia (condoms, lube, toys, etc.)

Working or Living Conditions
- Not free to leave or come and go as they wish
- Under 18 and providing commercial sex acts
- Is in the commercial sex industry and has a pimp or a manager
- Is unpaid, underpaid, or paid only through tips
- Works excessively long and/or unusual hours
- Is not allowed breaks or has other unusual restrictions while at work
- Owes a large debt and is unable to pay it
- Was recruited through false promises

---

1. Kyra Doubek, "Survivor Leaders from around the World Share Their Stories with UN Ambassadors," Online UN Conference, July 30, 2021.
2. Human Trafficking in Our Backyard, "Recognizing the Signs," https://inourbackyard.org/the-issue/indicators-for-ht/. See also Washington Trafficking Prevention, "2021 TCCAT Community Conversation," February 1, 2021, https://www.youtube.com/watch?v=hufL1R29xbQ.

- Works or lives in a location with high security measures (opaque or boarded-up windows, barbed wire, security cameras, etc.)

Poor Mental Health or Abnormal Behavior

- Is fearful, anxious, depressed, submissive, tense, nervous, or paranoid
- Exhibits fearful or anxious behavior if law enforcement is mentioned
- Avoids eye contact
- Poor physical health
- Lacks access to healthcare
- Appears malnourished
- Shows signs of physical and/or sexual abuse, physical restraint, confinement, or torture

Lack of Control

- Has few or no personal possessions
- Is not in control of their own money/has no access to financial records or institutions
- Lacks access to their own identification documents (passport, driver's license, or other personal ID)
- Is not allowed or able to speak for themselves (a third party always present, insistent on translating)

Other

- Inability to clarify residence address; claims to be "just visiting" relatives or friends
- Lack of knowledge of whereabouts; does not know what city/state they are in
- Has no sense of time
- Stories have numerous inconsistencies

It is important to learn to identify red flags that indicate the possibility that someone in your community could be a victim or perpetrator of human trafficking. If you see red flags, do not intervene yourself. Engaging a victim or perpetrator directly could put you or the victim in danger. Instead, contact your local police, or call the U.S. human trafficking hotline: 888.373.7888. For more important resources, refer to Appendix C (page 143).

CLOSING

This week, ask Jesus to shine light into the shadows of your life and your community. Ask the Lord to help you see what you may not have previously recognized. If the Lord reveals shadows in your life, surrender these places to God.

Consider using the following prayer that we will end with today. This prayer was originally written by Israel's King David, who learned firsthand the destructive nature of darkness and also the Lord's readiness to forgive him when David chose to repent and face the truth. Next week, we'll unpack a dark point in David's story.

Close your time together by praying **Psalm 139:23–24**: *Search me, God, and know my heart; test me and know my anxious thoughts. See if there is any offensive way in me, and lead me in the way everlasting.*

Biblical Application of Lesson 3

DAY 1

It may be easy to read through a story or a chapter of the Bible and skip over the meaning within a single verse, but sometimes the significance is in the details.

Read **Genesis 35:22a**. (Note that in Genesis 35:10, God gave the name Israel to Jacob.)

²²*While Israel was living in that region, Reuben went in and slept with his father's concubine Bilhah, and Israel heard of it.*

1. What happened in this verse?

   _____

   _____

   _____

   _____

2. Who knew that the incident occurred?

   _____

   _____

3. Who is Reuben, and what was his special position in the family? (Refer to Genesis 35:23 if you aren't sure.)

   _____

   _____

   _____

   _____

In Jewish culture, the firstborn son is given special recognition in the family. A firstborn son's birthright is secured in Scripture and cannot be revoked by parental preference or family favoritism.

Read **Deuteronomy 21:15–17**:

15If a man has two wives, and he loves one but not the other, and both bear him sons but the firstborn is the son of the wife he does not love, 16when he wills his property to his sons, he must not give the rights of the firstborn to the son of the wife he loves in preference to his actual firstborn, the son of the wife he does not love. 17He must acknowledge the son of his unloved wife as the firstborn by giving him a double share of all he has. That son is the first sign of his father's strength. The right of the firstborn belongs to him.

4. How is the presented scenario similar to Reuben's family?

5. What rights does Reuben have under the law?

What initially appears to be an insignificant verse lays the groundwork for a powerful demonstration of God's response to unrepentant perpetrators.

Biblical Application of Lesson 3
DAY 2

Read **Genesis 48**.

1. What happened in this scene (pay special attention to verses 1–5, 9, 15–16, 18–19, and 21)?

   _____

   _____

   _____

   _____

   _____

   _____

2. Which son did Jacob award the birthright blessing to in this chapter, and which grandsons did he adopt as his own sons so they could each receive a blessing and an inheritance?

   _____

   _____

   _____

   _____

   _____

   _____

After the birthright blessing, Jacob summoned all his sons to gather so he could bless them and their descendants.

Read **Genesis 49:3–4**:
³Reuben, you are my firstborn,
my might, the first sign of my strength,
excelling in honor, excelling in power.
⁴Turbulent as the waters, you will no longer excel,
for you went up onto your father's bed,
onto my couch and defiled it.

3. Now, who was aware of Reuben's crime? How was Reuben held accountable? What did it cost him?

4. What do you think Bilhah's sons, Dan and Naphtali, could be thinking about their brother Reuben?

Biblical Application of Lesson 3
DAY 3

Read 1 Chronicles 5:1–2:

¹*The sons of Reuben the firstborn of Israel (he was the firstborn, but when he defiled his father's marriage bed, his rights as firstborn were given to the sons of Joseph son of Israel; so he could not be listed in the genealogical record in accordance with his birthright, ²and though Judah was the strongest of his brothers and a ruler came from him, the rights of the firstborn belonged to Joseph).*

In case the Genesis chapters were confusing to anyone, 1 Chronicles clears up any remaining questions about Reuben and his birthright: he lost it when Jacob died. Scholars have noted that Reuben essentially disappears from prominence when the twelve tribes are discussed in Israelite history.

1. We don't have any stories of Reuben sinning in Genesis other than his rape of Bilhah. How does it affect your perception of God's vision of justice to know that Reuben was punished so severely for this crime?

   _____

   _____

   _____

   _____

   _____

   _____

   _____

   _____

   _____

2. What might be the ripple effect through the generations of Reuben's family for him to have lost his birthright?

_____

_____

_____

_____

_____

_____

_____

3. If Reuben lost his birthright over his crime against Bilhah, why didn't the birthright go to the next son in line? Joseph was the eleventh son—why did it go to him?

_____

_____

_____

_____

_____

_____

Biblical Application of Lesson 3
DAY 4

Genesis 37 records that Joseph's ten older brothers became so jealous of him that they devised a plan to sell him into slavery.

1. In modern-day terms, what did Joseph's brothers do to him?

   _____
   _____
   _____
   _____
   _____

2. What are some reasons why Joseph's other brothers may have each forfeited their chance to receive the birthright after Reuben lost it?

   _____
   _____
   _____
   _____
   _____
   _____

Scripture does not explicitly record why Jacob skipped all the brothers ahead of Joseph in the birth order, but what is clear is that giving Joseph the birthright places Joseph over all of his brothers.

3. Write down a few things that stood out to you about God's response to injustice as you studied this week's scriptures and stories.

4. How might these passages help inform a Christian response to modern-day sexual assault and trafficking?

LESSON 4

"See if There Is Any Offensive Way in Me . . ."

■ Organizing Principle

A Christian approach invites perpetrators to a place of conviction rather than condemnation.

■ Learning Objectives

- Distinguish differences between God's response to perpetrators compared to God's response to victims.
- Discover the role of the abuse of power in cases of sexual assault and exploitation.
- Learners will practice shifting evaluative focus to the perpetrator rather than the victim.

OPENING PRAYER

Ask someone to pray briefly for the group and for this session.

FEELINGS IDENTIFICATION

Locate the Feeling Wheel at the back of the book (page 140). Take a moment to examine the wheel and identify how you are currently feeling.

When you are ready, share one or two words from the wheel that represent how you are feeling right now. Do not explain the words you chose or comment on the words that others share.

DEBRIEF THE WEEK

Share with one another what you have been processing since the last meeting, considering prior discussion and any engagement you did with the mid-week biblical application lessons. Trauma-related content can be difficult to process and discuss. This time is meant to give participants a chance to process recent content before introducing this week's topic.

LEARN TOGETHER

Have you ever apologized to someone before you knew what you were sorry for? When we do something wrong, it is important to apologize, but an apology means little if we don't understand what we did wrong.

When we say sorry before knowing what we did, what are we actually sorry about? Are we sorry for getting in trouble? Are we sorry for making the other person mad? Neither of these reasons get to the heart of the actual offense, and both could lead to unhealthy ways of covering up future offenses.

If we restrict ourselves to only being sorry for getting caught, we may become better at hiding our offenses. If we allow ourselves to only be sorry for making someone else mad, then we may attempt to manipulate others' moods in order to deter them from becoming upset with us, even when we have actually harmed them. These are only two of the many negative outcomes that can occur when we do not take the time to recognize what we have done wrong and sincerely attempt to make things right.

It is important to be honest with ourselves when we sin against the Lord. If we do not recognize what we have done wrong, we can get caught up in misunderstanding why

God is convicting us. It's not about not getting caught, or not making God mad. First, we must bring our darkness into the light. Only then can we feel a proper remorse that can lead to a change of behavior.

Today we will dive into details often overlooked in a popular biblical story that has to do with various forms of the abuse of power. Our goal is to examine the layers of wrongdoing for the purpose of better understanding that God, who is both compassionate and just, extends the same forgiveness to us if we choose to receive it.

Scripture and Discussion

Read **2 Samuel 11** together:

¹*In the spring of the year, the time when kings go out to battle, David sent Joab with his officers and all Israel with him; they ravaged the Ammonites and besieged Rabbah. But David remained at Jerusalem.*

²*It happened, late one afternoon when David rose from his couch and was walking about on the roof of the king's house, that he saw from the roof a woman bathing; the woman was very beautiful.* ³*David sent someone to inquire about the woman. It was reported, "This is Bathsheba daughter of Eliam, the wife of Uriah the Hittite."* ⁴*So David sent messengers to get her, and she came to him, and he lay with her. (Now she was purifying herself after her period.) Then she returned to her house.* ⁵*The woman conceived, and she sent and told David, "I am pregnant."*

⁶*So David sent word to Joab, "Send me Uriah the Hittite." And Joab sent Uriah to David.* ⁷*When Uriah came to him, David asked how Joab and the people fared and how the war was going.* ⁸*Then David said to Uriah, "Go down to your house and wash your feet." Uriah went out of the king's house, and there followed him a present from the king.* ⁹*But Uriah slept at the entrance of the king's house with all the servants of his lord and did not go down to his house.* ¹⁰*When they told David, "Uriah did not go down to his house," David said to Uriah, "You have just come from a journey. Why did you not go down to your house?"* ¹¹*Uriah said to David, "The ark and Israel and Judah remain in booths, and my lord Joab and the servants of my lord are camping in the open field; shall I then go to my house to eat and to drink and to lie with my wife? As you live and as your soul lives, I will not do such a thing."* ¹²*Then David said to Uriah, "Remain here today also, and tomorrow I will send you back." So Uriah remained in Jerusalem that day. On the next day,* ¹³*David invited him to eat and drink in his pres-*

ence and made him drunk, and in the evening he went out to lie on his couch with the servants of his lord, but he did not go down to his house.

[14]In the morning David wrote a letter to Joab and sent it by the hand of Uriah. [15]In the letter he wrote, "Set Uriah in the forefront of the hardest fighting, and then draw back from him, so that he may be struck down and die." [16]As Joab kept watch over the city, he assigned Uriah to the place where he knew there were valiant warriors. [17]The men of the city came out and fought with Joab, and some of the servants of David among the people fell. Uriah the Hittite was killed as well. [18]Then Joab sent and told David all the news about the fighting, [19]and he instructed the messenger, "When you have finished telling the king all the news about the fighting, [20]if the king's anger rises and if he says to you, 'Why did you go so near the city to fight? Did you not know that they would shoot from the wall? [21]Who killed Abimelech son of Jerubbaal? Did not a woman throw an upper millstone on him from the wall, so that he died at Thebez? Why did you go so near the wall?' then you shall say, 'Your servant Uriah the Hittite is dead, too.'"

[22]So the messenger went and came and told David all that Joab had sent him to tell. [23]The messenger said to David, "The men gained an advantage over us and came out against us in the field, but we drove them back to the entrance of the gate. [24]Then the archers shot at your servants from the wall; some of the king's servants are dead, and your servant Uriah the Hittite is dead also." [25]David said to the messenger, "Thus you shall say to Joab, 'Do not let this matter trouble you, for the sword devours now one and now another; press your attack on the city and overthrow it.' And encourage him."

[26]When the wife of Uriah heard that her husband was dead, she made lamentation for him. [27]When the mourning was over, David sent and brought her to his house, and she became his wife and bore him a son.

But the thing that David had done displeased the Lord. (NRSVUE)

Even though this scripture often refers to David and Bathsheba together, we will be discussing each person separately. The extended study this week is dedicated to learning what Scripture tells us about Bathsheba. Today we will focus only on David's actions.

1. How did David neglect his royal leadership responsibilities? (Important context: Kings often led their troops into battle themselves.)

_____

_____

_____

_____

2. Regardless of whether the act with Bathsheba is categorized as adultery (making both David and Bathsheba guilty of sin) or sexual assault (making David alone responsible for the offense against Bathsheba), King David broke the Lord's seventh and tenth commandments. What are these commandments? (See Exodus 20:14; 17)

_____

_____

_____

_____

3. When David asked who the woman was, he received an answer that should have stopped him in his tracks. Look up the following verses to understand the significance of his servant's response. (Important context: David's mighty men were a group of soldiers who stuck with David through thick and thin, before he was king and also throughout his reign.) Who were Bathsheba's father, Eliam, and her husband, Uriah? (See 2 Samuel 23, starting with verse 8.)

_____

_____

_____

_____

4. When David learned he had impregnated Bathsheba, how did he attempt to use Uriah to cover up his crime, and how did it backfire? (Focus on 2 Samuel 11:8–13)

_____
_____
_____
_____
_____

5. When he couldn't get Uriah to go to his own home and sleep with his own wife, Bathsheba, David decided to have Uriah killed in the front lines of battle (and had Uriah unknowingly carry his own death warrant back to his commanding officer). David treats everyone in this story as a pawn he can use to achieve his sinful aim of covering up his crime with Bathsheba. Describe how each person's humanity is ignored or dismissed in David's dealings with them.

   Bathsheba:

_____
_____
_____
_____
_____

Uriah:

_____
_____
_____
_____
_____

Joab:

_____

_____

_____

_____

_____

6. Joab's lack of knowledge of the situation and of David's larger aims become clear when Joab gives specific instructions to a messenger about how to communicate to David the enormous losses they suffered in the battle that killed Uriah. Joab expected David to be angry about the news. Consider the contrast between the king's expected response (2 Samuel 11:18–21) and his actual response (2 Samuel 11:22–25). What do you notice?

_____

_____

_____

_____

_____

Trafficking and Discussion

Today we have purposefully focused on David's actions. Although King David was not a human trafficker, he serves as a clear biblical example of someone who used his power to abuse Bathsheba and have Uriah killed.

When we focus on the perpetrator's actions, then the concerning actions are easier to recognize, even if the person doing the harm may not fit into our stereotypes, assumptions, or preconceived notions about what a perpetrator should look like.

1. How have you previously heard the David and Bathsheba story interpreted or explained?

_____

_____

_____

_____

_____

2. How has your view of the 2 Samuel story changed with the focus placed on David's actions?

_____

_____

_____

_____

_____

One of the most difficult parts of discussing human trafficking is learning to make the perpetrator visible. There would be no trafficking victims if there were no buyers or traffickers! Statistics say there are an estimated 40 to 180 sex buyers for every *one* CSE survivor. If this is the case, where are they? Now that we are learning how to identify what trafficking looks like in the local community, we can learn to break our stereotypes in order to see victims, traffickers, and buyers within our own communities.

Local communities tend to have a difficult time talking about the presence of perpetrators. Either we do not want to acknowledge that they exist within the community, or we want to punish them to the fullest extent of the law, and then some. Trafficking survivors often feel shocked and confused by the volatile responses they receive from the local community. From a survivor perspective, the community may appear to ignore or even harbor perpetrators. Often, survivors share stories of not being believed when they have tried to tell a community member that someone who does not fit the stereotypical abuser profile has abused them. They might be told they are mistaken, or they might be accused of trying to destroy the reputation of a good person.

Once evidence of abuse becomes undeniable within a community, the tables often turn very quickly. The perpetrator is perceived and treated by the community as a monster more so than a criminal. Although anger is understandable in these situations, community outrage often leads to unrealistic or problematic solutions. Common statements may include, "Kill them all," or, "Lock them up and throw away the key," or, "Throw them in with the murderers." When community members can begin to recognize that perpetrators are real humans often living lives that appear to be totally normal, instead of monsters lurking in alleyways, then we can create appropriate space to believe victims and survivors, acknowledge the reality of abuse, and hold perpetrators accountable in ways that convict rather than condemn them.

3. Why do you think community members exhibit two opposing views about perpetrators (denial of their existence, then outrage)?

_____

_____

_____

_____

4. How might these conflicting community views ultimately work against the efforts of trafficking prevention and awareness?

_____

_____

_____

_____

_____

_____

5. Where can perpetrators get help? (Communities who may have resources for trafficking survivors often have little to no resources for helping perpetrators get out of the industry.)

_____

_____

_____

_____

_____

_____

_____

_____

Even though CSE is on the rise, sex traffickers and buyers often remain anonymous. The anti-trafficking movement is working to shift scrutiny away from victims and toward perpetrators. This shift is proving successful. More community members are learning what trafficking looks like and contacting authorities to step in. In the case of King David, let's read who stepped in to hold David accountable.

Read **2 Samuel 12:1–14** together:

¹*And the* Lord *sent Nathan to David. He came to him and said to him, "There were two men in a certain city, the one rich and the other poor.* ²*The rich man had very many flocks and herds,* ³*but the poor man had nothing but one little ewe lamb that he had bought. He brought it up, and it grew up with him and with his children; it used to eat of his meager fare and drink from his cup and lie in his bosom, and it was like a daughter to him.* ⁴*Now there came a traveler to the rich man, and he was loath to take one of his own flock or herd to prepare for the wayfarer who had come to him, but he took the poor man's lamb and prepared that for the guest who had come to him."* ⁵*Then David's anger was greatly kindled against the man. He said to Nathan, "As the* Lord *lives, the man who has done this deserves to die;* ⁶*he shall restore the lamb fourfold because he did this thing and because he had no pity."*

⁷Nathan said to David, "You are the man! Thus says the Lord, the God of Israel: I anointed you king over Israel, and I rescued you from the hand of Saul; ⁸I gave you your master's house and your master's wives into your bosom and gave you the house of Israel and of Judah, and if that had been too little, I would have added as much more. ⁹Why have you despised the word of the Lord, to do what is evil in his sight? You have struck down Uriah the Hittite with the sword and have taken his wife to be your wife and have killed him with the sword of the Ammonites. ¹⁰Now, therefore, the sword shall never depart from your house, for you have despised me and have taken the wife of Uriah the Hittite to be your wife. ¹¹Thus says the Lord: I will raise up trouble against you from within your own house, and I will take your wives before your eyes and give them to your neighbor, and he shall lie with your wives in broad daylight. ¹²For you did it secretly, but I will do this thing before all Israel and in broad daylight." ¹³David said to Nathan, "I have sinned against the Lord." Nathan said to David, "Now the Lord has put away your sin; you shall not die. ¹⁴Nevertheless, because by this deed you have utterly scorned the Lord, the child born to you shall die." (NRSVUE)

The prophet Nathan confronted the king in a clever way that allowed him to experience empathy, kingly responsibility, and a desire for justice before convicting David's own actions.

Local communities need more Nathans. Nathan led David toward conviction instead of condemnation.

1. What do you think is the difference between conviction and condemnation?

_____

_____

_____

_____

_____

_____

_____

2. How did Nathan offer dignity to Uriah and Bathsheba while convicting David?

3. How did David ultimately respond?

Even though David repented and received forgiveness from God, David and Bathsheba's baby still died. Scripture indicates that this was a punishment for David, but it can be difficult for us to stomach because Bathsheba and her baby—the primary victims of this "punishment"—did nothing wrong (notice that neither Nathan nor God convict Bathsheba or the baby in this story—only David sinned here).

4. What parallels about unintended consequences and innocent victims can be drawn between this punishment for David's actions and the problem of human trafficking today?

_____

_____

_____

_____

_____

_____

_____

5. Common misinterpretations of this story include people drawing the incorrect conclusion that the baby's death occurred because of sexual sin, or because the child was conceived *before* Bathsheba was David's wife. What dangerous implications do distortions like these have for our conceptions of God and how God views children who were conceived by sexual assault, adultery, or out of wedlock? Why should we work against these misinterpretations?

_____

_____

_____

_____

_____

_____

_____

6. The reason God gives for David's punishment is that David "utterly scorned the LORD" (v. 14). How have David's actions throughout this whole story demonstrated his scorn (or contempt, or lack of respect) for God?

_____
_____
_____
_____
_____
_____
_____

7. Beyond feeling a general grief over his son's death (something everyone can relate to), what other implications were there in David's son dying? (Think about the culture of the time, the traditional mode of succession, etc.)

_____
_____
_____
_____
_____
_____
_____

CLOSING

In David's story, we see a perpetrator who repented of his sins. Remember that the same invitation is granted to us when we do wrong. God seeks to convict us rather than condemn us.

Conviction, like in a healthy relationship between a parent and a child, invites us to stand before the Lord and recognize what we have done wrong. We may feel remorse or a deep sense of regret for our actions as we, like David, confront what we have done. If we are willing, remorse can lead us to repentance, which is a commitment to change our actions. It's never too late to ask for forgiveness from the Lord and stop the patterns of our harmful actions.

This week, use David's prayer of remorse and repentance, found in Psalm 51, to meet with the Lord.

Throughout this study, you may have been wondering why David is called an adulterer if the act against Bathsheba was rape? This topic, along with taking a closer look at Bathsheba, is the focus of the mid-week content.

Next week, we will study an even clearer account of rape and the revenge that ensues.

Close your time together by praying these excerpts from **Psalm 51** (verses 1–2, 10–13): *Have mercy on me, O God, according to your unfailing love; according to your great compassion blot out my transgressions. Wash away all my iniquity and cleanse me from my sin. Create in me a pure heart, O God, and renew a steadfast spirit within me. Do not cast me from your presence or take your Holy Spirit from me. Restore to me the joy of your salvation and grant me a willing spirit, to sustain me. Then I will teach transgressors your ways, so that sinners will turn back to you.*

Biblical Application of Lesson 4
DAY 1

A focus of interpretation of David and Bathsheba's story has, for generations, been the narrative that they had an "affair." No legitimate interpretation has ever condoned David's actions, but this story has been the source of much debate over Bathsheba's innocence in the matter. Let's examine what we can learn about Bathsheba and her actions from Scripture.

Read **Leviticus 15:18–19**:

[18]When a man has sexual relations with a woman and there is an emission of semen, both of them must bathe with water, and they will be unclean till evening.

[19]When a woman has her regular flow of blood, the impurity of her monthly period will last seven days, and anyone who touches her will be unclean till evening.

1. Why might Bathsheba have been bathing in the first place, and why was she in sight of the king? (It is a common mistake to think that Bathsheba was bathing on a roof, but that is not what Scripture says. Her location is not recorded, but we are told in 2 Samuel 11:2 who *is* on a roof.)

_____

_____

_____

_____

_____

_____

Read 2 Samuel 11:4:

⁴Then David sent messengers to get her. She came to him, and he slept with her. (Now she was purifying herself from her monthly uncleanness.)

2. Verse 4 leaves the question open about Bathsheba's menstruation cycle, and scholars are divided on what it means. Is it talking about her washing according to the law after having sexual relations with David? Or is it referring to why she was bathing before David sent for her? We can't be sure. Since Scripture does mention "her monthly uncleanness," let's assume it's talking about her reason for bathing when David first saw her. Why might it be significant to record a detail that implies that Bathsheba has just finished her menstrual cycle? (Hint: think about what menstruation means as related to pregnancy, and the lengths David eventually went to in an attempt to cover up his sin.)

   _____
   _____
   _____
   _____

3. Why would Bathsheba go to the palace? Could her agreeing to go be a sign of consent? (Look at what the passage tells us: David sent messengers to escort her there. Think about what kind of agency she may or may not have had.)

   _____
   _____
   _____
   _____
   _____

4. Consider further the context that Bathsheba's father and husband—both members of David's mighty men—were away at war. Why might Bathsheba go with the king's messengers, during a war that her male family members were fighting in, if they told her she had been summoned to see the king at the palace?

_____

_____

_____

_____

_____

_____

_____

Biblical Application of Lesson 4
DAY 2

Was what happened to Bathsheba considered rape by biblical standards? It all depends on how a certain passage in Deuteronomy is interpreted and applied to the 2 Samuel story.

Read **Deuteronomy 22:23–27**:

²³*If a man happens to meet in a town a virgin pledged to be married and he sleeps with her,* ²⁴*you shall take both of them to the gate of that town and stone them to death—the young woman because she was in a town and did not scream for help, and the man because he violated another man's wife. You must purge the evil from among you.*

²⁵*But if out in the country a man happens to meet a young woman pledged to be married and rapes her, only the man who has done this shall die.* ²⁶*Do nothing to the woman; she has committed no sin deserving death. This case is like that of someone who attacks and murders a neighbor,* ²⁷*for the man found the young woman out in the country, and though the betrothed woman screamed, there was no one to rescue her.*

According to this passage, rape occurs when a woman is sexually assaulted by a man who is not her husband. Also according to this passage, the woman is required to scream in order to avoid being seen as a willing participant in the sin. If they are in a town and the woman does not scream for help, then she is considered equally at fault. If they are in the country, the woman is automatically deemed innocent because the assumption is that she screamed and nobody heard.

1. Second Samuel does not tell us whether Bathsheba screamed for help. Even if she had screamed when David advanced on her, what do you think would have happened? How likely was she to be rescued from the king?

   _____
   _____
   _____

2. The law in Deuteronomy 22 takes the presence or absence of community members into account. What might this portion of the law imply about the responsibility of community members taking action when an assault takes place?

3. Some scholars surmise that a location like the king's bedroom would more closely align with the countryside interpretation in Deuteronomy, since persons close enough to hear a scream would likely be unable to respond. What are your thoughts?

Biblical Application of Lesson 4
DAY 3

Regardless of whether what happened between David and Bathsheba was rape by biblical standards, we can certainly affirm that it was rape by modern-day standards. The story tells us that David didn't even know who Bathsheba was before he saw her bathing.

1. Why does their being complete strangers before this story matter? (Think about conditions for adultery and affairs.)

   _____
   _____
   _____
   _____

Additionally, the issue of power dynamics indicts him most clearly. In the relationship between a king and his subjects, the king has all the power.

2. Why does the power dynamic mean that Bathsheba was unquestionably a victim of rape, especially by modern standards? (Consider the issues of agency and consent. Return to the legal definition of trafficking if that is helpful.)

   _____
   _____
   _____
   _____

3. Consider once more the case of Abraham trafficking Sarah to both Pharaoh and Abimelek. In the eyes of God, would Sarah have been an adulteress or a victim if they had slept with her?

_____

_____

_____

_____

_____

_____

_____

4. It could be argued that, as king, David had the right to add another woman (concubine or mistress or wife) to his harem. Yet there are clues in 2 Samuel 11 that indicate this event was a single act rather than the start of an official relationship. What are those clues? (Consider, among other things, both of their actions in the aftermath.)

_____

_____

_____

_____

_____

_____

_____

Biblical Application of Lesson 4
DAY 4

When the prophet Nathan confronted David with his sin, he did not hold back. Further, he did not place any guilt on Bathsheba for David's actions. Rather, he compared her to a beloved lamb who was slaughtered and eaten by the king for reasons of pure selfishness and greed.

1. Who else does the Bible compare to a slaughtered lamb? (Check out **Isaiah 53:7**; **Acts 8:32–35**; and **Revelation 5:6**)

   _____

   _____

   _____

   _____

   _____

   _____

   _____

Likewise, God also did not hold Bathsheba responsible for David's sin against her. Even though her first child with David died, she went on to have others. We cannot know for sure if they intentionally honored the prophet who convicted David for his sins, but one of Bathsheba's additional sons with David was named Nathan (see 1 Chronicles 3:5).

Many scholars consider the most redemptive part of Bathsheba's story to be her appearance in the official records of the lineage of Jesus Christ. Prophets foretold that the Messiah would come from the line of David. Even though David had many wives and concubines, God chose to have Bathsheba bear the genealogical line of the Messiah—twice, depending on which Gospel you read.

2. Jesus's heritage is recorded in **Matthew 1:1–16** and **Luke 3:23–38**. Who was David's descendant with Bathsheba according to Matthew? Who was David's descendant with Bathsheba according to Luke?

3. Why might it be important for Bathsheba's story, and her dignity, to be considered so important as to be recorded in Jesus's genealogical line?

LESSON 5

Vigilantes: Heroes or Villains?

■ Organizing Principle

A Christian response to commercial sexual exploitation (CSE) does not repay evil for evil.

■ Learning Objectives

- Differentiate between a theatrical and a realistic approach to CSE.
- Recognize that vigilantes negatively impact community awareness, attitudes, and responses to victims and perpetrators of sexual assault and exploitation.
- Examine the overlap between pornography, sex addiction, and CSE.

OPENING PRAYER

Ask someone to pray briefly for the group and for this session.

FEELINGS IDENTIFICATION

Locate the Feeling Wheel at the back of the book (page 140). Take a moment to examine the wheel and identify how you are currently feeling.

When you are ready, share one or two words from the wheel that represent how you are feeling right now. Do not explain the words you chose or comment on the words that others share.

DEBRIEF THE WEEK

Share with one another what you have been processing since the last meeting, considering prior discussion and any engagement you did with the mid-week biblical application lessons. Trauma-related content can be difficult to process and discuss. This time is meant to give participants a chance to process recent content before introducing this week's topic.

LEARN TOGETHER

Action is one of the most popular movie genres. Who doesn't love to see the hero beat the villain, especially when the heroes are justly avenging either themselves or others for the wrongs done by the villains? Yet Scripture says we are not meant to repay evil for evil (Romans 12:17) and that vengeance is God's alone (Romans 12:19).

So why do action movies featuring vigilante heroes feel so inspiring? The hero has broken societal rules, and society must choose whether their actions were justifiable. The story feels good because the villains are despicable enough for the audience to grant license to the hero to wreak havoc all over the world in order to defeat the villain. The victims are rescued, the villain is defeated, the hero is pardoned, and the audience feels they have witnessed and rooted for good in the world.

Far before vigilantes dominated United States pop culture, the Bible recorded several accounts of vengeance enacted as a response to initial acts of injustice. Today we will focus on a classic case of rape and revenge, but rather than focusing on the act of sexual assault itself, we will scrutinize some of the actions of other characters in the story to remind ourselves not to make the familiar mistake of exonerating vigilantes by justifying evil being repaid for evil.

Do Christians generally regard these characters as heroes or villains in the biblical account? The way these passages are discussed will shape the attitudes and responses of today's listeners as they approach Scripture, movies, and real-life violence.

Scripture and Discussion

Read **2 Samuel 13:1–29** together:

¹*Some time later, David's son Amnon fell in love with Tamar the beautiful sister of Absalom, who was also David's son. ²Amnon was so upset over his half sister that he made himself sick. She was a virgin, and it seemed impossible in Amnon's view to do anything to her. ³But Amnon had a very clever friend named Jonadab, who was David's brother Shimeah's son.*

⁴*"Prince," Jonadab said to him, "why are you so down, morning after morning? Tell me about it."*

So Amnon told him, "I'm in love with Tamar, the sister of my brother Absalom."

⁵*"Lie down on your bed and pretend to be sick," Jonadab said to him. "When your father comes to see you, tell him, 'Please let my sister Tamar come and give me some food to eat. Let her prepare the food in my sight so I can watch and eat from her own hand.'"*

⁶*So Amnon lay down and pretended to be sick. The king came to see him, and Amnon told the king, "Please let my sister Tamar come and make a couple of heart-shaped cakes in front of me so I can eat from her hand."*

⁷*David sent word to Tamar at the palace: "Please go to your brother Amnon's house and prepare some food for him."*

⁸*So Tamar went to her brother Amnon's house where he was lying down. She took dough, kneaded it, made heart-shaped cakes in front of him, and then cooked them.* ⁹*She took the pan and served Amnon, but he refused to eat.*

"Everyone leave me," Amnon said. So everyone left him. ¹⁰*Then Amnon said to Tamar, "Bring the food into the bedroom so I can eat from your hand." So Tamar took the heart-shaped cakes she had made and brought them to her brother Amnon in the bedroom.* ¹¹*When she served him the food, he grabbed her and said, "Come have sex with me, my sister."*

¹²*But she said to him, "No, my brother! Don't rape me. Such a thing shouldn't be done in Israel. Don't do this horrible thing.* ¹³*Think about me—where could I hide my shame? And you—you would become like some fool in Israel! Please, just talk to the king! He won't keep me from marrying you."*

¹⁴But Amnon refused to listen to her. He was stronger than she was, and so he raped her.

¹⁵But then Amnon felt intense hatred for her. In fact, his hatred for her was greater than the love he had felt for her. So Amnon told her, "Get out of here!"

¹⁶"No, my brother!" she said. "Sending me away would be worse than the wrong you've already done."

But Amnon wouldn't listen to her. ¹⁷He summoned his young servant and said, "Get this woman out of my presence and lock the door after her." (¹⁸She was wearing a long-sleeved robe because that was what the virgin princesses wore as garments.) So Amnon's servant put her out and locked the door after her.

¹⁹Tamar put ashes on her head and tore the long-sleeved robe she was wearing. She put her hand on her head and walked away, crying as she went.

²⁰Her brother Absalom said to her, "Has your brother Amnon been with you? Keep quiet about it for now, sister; he's your brother. Don't let it bother you." So Tamar, a broken woman, lived in her brother Absalom's house.

²¹When King David heard about all this he got very angry, but he refused to punish his son Amnon because he loved him as his oldest child. ²²Absalom never spoke to Amnon, good word or bad, because he hated him for raping his sister Tamar.

²³Two years later, Absalom was shearing sheep at Baal-hazor near Ephraim, and he invited all the king's sons. ²⁴Absalom approached the king and said, "Your servant is shearing sheep. Would the king and his advisors please join me?"

²⁵But the king said to Absalom, "No, my son. We shouldn't all go, or we would be a burden on you." Although Absalom urged him, the king wasn't willing to go, although he gave Absalom a blessing.

²⁶Then Absalom said, "If you won't come, then let my brother Amnon go with us."

"Why should he go with you?" they asked him. ²⁷But Absalom urged him until he sent Amnon and all the other princes. Then Absalom made a banquet fit for a king.

²⁸Absalom commanded his servants, "Be on the lookout! When Amnon is happy with wine and I tell you to strike Amnon down, then kill him! Don't be afraid, because I my-self am giving you the order. Be brave and strong men." ²⁹So Absalom's servants did

to Amnon just what he had commanded. Then all the princes got up, jumped onto their mules, and fled. (CEB)

1. Describe the trap Amnon set for Tamar.

___

2. How did Amnon manipulate the community (his father, King David; servants; and other observers) to convince them that Tamar would not be in danger with him?

___

3. After Tamar was raped, what did she do, and where did she go?

___

4. What was Absalom's response to Tamar's rape?

Killing his brother wasn't enough for Absalom in his pursuit of justice and vengeance for his sister. Absalom also sought revenge against his father, King David. In his attempts to overthrow the king, Absalom raped David's concubines and rose up against his father in military battle. King David's general eventually murdered Absalom against David's explicit instructions (see 2 Samuel 16 and 18).

5. In these stories, usually Amnon is portrayed as a rapist and Absalom as a hero. How should Absalom be portrayed, taking into account the events of 2 Samuel 16?

6. What might sexual assault victims and perpetrators assume about God and the church when the biblical accounts are told in a way that skews toward portraying Absalom as a hero?

_____

_____

_____

_____

_____

_____

7. How does our culture predispose us to think the rape of Tamar (a virgin) is worse than the rape of David's concubines (not virgins)?

_____

_____

_____

_____

_____

_____

8. How does our culture predispose us to condemn some sex crimes (such as Amnon's) and justify or ignore others (such as Absalom's)?

_____

_____

_____

_____

_____

_____

Trafficking and Discussion

In 2008, the U.S. action thriller *Taken* was released. It was a blockbuster hit that remains popular today, and it's easy to see why. Liam Neeson's character is every parent's fantasy of who they themselves would want to be if their own child were kidnapped and trafficked. In his famous monologue as he speaks to the kidnapper on the phone, he says:

> I don't know who you are. I don't know what you want. If you are looking for ransom, I can tell you I don't have money. But what I do have are a very particular set of skills—skills I have acquired over a very long career, skills that make me a nightmare for people like you. If you let my daughter go now, that'll be the end of it. I will not look for you; I will not pursue you. But if you don't, I will look for you, I will find you, and I will kill you.

This powerful speech ignites an action-packed thriller that, in 2008, put the topic of sex trafficking on the radar for the general population. But you might be surprised to find out that many trafficking survivors disliked the movie. Since the movie introduced so many viewers to the crime of CSE for the first time, the uninformed often assume that CSE generally occurs in the manner in which it was portrayed onscreen.[1] In response to growing myths about trafficking, survivors have explained that movies like this distort the trafficking recruitment process, making it seem like sexual exploitation is a foreign enterprise that targets unsuspecting, young, U.S. girls when it actually targets and victimizes all kinds of people in all kinds of countries.[2] These storylines often erase the plight of the fictional victims, who remain side characters in the shadows of the main action heroes who wage war on anyone who stands in their way.

When a movie like *Taken* forms the general population's initial awareness of the crime of commercial sexual exploitation, these faulty concepts may become the only perspective from which the population builds its impression of trafficking victims, perpetrators, and heroes. The reality is that Liam Neeson's character does not exist, and anyone who attempted to take justice into their own hands in the same way he did would be prosecuted.

---

1. Jonathan Todres, "Movies and Myths about Human Trafficking," *The Conversation*, January 20, 2016, https://theconversation.com/movies-and-myths-about-human-trafficking-51300.
2. See Andrea J. Nichols, Tonya Edmond, and Erin C. Heil, eds, *Social Work Practice with Survivors of Sex Trafficking and Commercial Sexual Exploitation* (New York: Columbia University Press, 2018).

If vigilante characters don't exist in real life, why are they such popular fictional characters? Movies like *Taken* capitalize on audience emotion. It may be that the general population has a vague understanding that trafficking is real and that it is disturbing, and wants to feel that something good is being accomplished. Rather than making a realistic difference by working to become anti-trafficking change makers in their communities, they settle for fictional portrayals of Robin Hood-like characters to open the door to the disturbance, kill the villains, and close the door behind them.

The danger of relying on action movies for our information about trafficking is that audiences begin to believe that vigilante justice is both possible and rational; that trafficking plays out exactly the way it was portrayed in the movie (and is therefore distant, random, and fairly uncommon); and that rescuing the victim equals resolution. These issues all complicate the real-life problem of trafficking, making it even more difficult for CSE survivors and anti-trafficking organizations to facilitate real awareness and action among the general population.

1. How does pop culture (including movies like *Taken*) shape our thoughts about trafficking victims? How does it shape our thoughts about perpetrators? How does it shape our thoughts about the role of parents of CSE victims?

___

___

___

___

2. As a group, consider a famous plot from a book, TV show, or movie where the hero's violent actions are justified by the characters in the movie, the message of the movie, or in the mind of the audience. In real life, what would be the penalty for these violent actions?

___

___

___

___

Looking back at scripture, let's turn our focus to Tamar. She can get lost in the details and reactions happening all around her, so let's give her a voice. Tamar didn't need a vigilante.

3. What might Tamar have wanted or needed in verses 18 and 19?

_____

_____

_____

_____

_____

_____

4. What might Tamar have wanted or needed in verses 21–23?

_____

_____

_____

_____

_____

_____

5. Just like Tamar, a trafficking victim or survivor doesn't need to be avenged by a vigilante. What might they need from the community instead?

_____

_____

_____

_____

_____

If commercial sexual exploitation in the local community doesn't look like the movie *Taken*, what does it look like instead?

- A boyfriend who needs a favor "just this once" to get a little money to hold him over; the pattern repeats, often with increased threats of abuse or exposure, trapping the victim
- Online pornography sites
- Companies that profit directly or indirectly from CSE (the National Center on Sexual Exploitation publishes an annual "Dirty Dozen" list of companies who are being held accountable for their role in CSE; the current list can be found at endsexualexploitation.org)
- Peers using threats to publicize sexting images or other forms of blackmail
- Family sex abuse and exploitation
- Any time a sex act against a minor is exchanged for any goods, food, or resources
- Any time a sex act against an adult is exchanged for any goods, food, or resources when force, fraud, or coercion has occurred.

6. With these scenarios in mind, what might a victim look like, and what might a trafficker look like?

_____
_____
_____
_____

7. What action could a community member noticing these red flags take?

_____
_____
_____
_____
_____

CLOSING

So far, we have focused mainly on women as victims of sexual assault and exploitation, but the Bible gives multiple accounts of men being the targets of victimization as well. We will wrap up our six-week study by learning about men next week.

Additionally, this week's mid-week content will delve into the issue of pornography and how it relates to sex trafficking. Regardless of whether you personally struggle with pornography, I encourage you to learn about this addiction that impacts people both inside and outside the church. The goal is to acknowledge an issue that is easy to ignore, to recognize addiction, and to learn about resources so that people who use pornography can get the help they need.

Close your time together by praying **Psalm 25:7–11** (NLT): *Do not remember the rebellious sins of my youth. Remember me in the light of your unfailing love, for you are merciful, O Lord. The Lord is good and does what is right; he shows the proper path to those who go astray. He leads the humble in doing right, teaching them his way. The Lord leads with unfailing love and faithfulness all who keep his covenant and obey his demands. For the honor of your name, O Lord, forgive my many, many sins.*

Biblical Application of Lesson 5
DAY 1

In the last two sessions, we have studied biblical accounts of sexual assault that began when the perpetrator treated the victim first as an object of lust and then as a target of their next steps. Objectification and forced actions—often present in sexual abuse and exploitation—are in direct opposition to the way God wants people to treat one another.

Read **Genesis 1:26–30**:

26Then God said, "Let us make mankind in our image, in our likeness, so that they may rule over the fish in the sea and the birds in the sky, over the livestock and all the wild animals, and over all the creatures that move along the ground."

27So God created mankind in his own image, in the image of God he created them; male and female he created them.

28God blessed them and said to them, "Be fruitful and increase in number; fill the earth and subdue it. Rule over the fish in the sea and the birds in the sky and over every living creature that moves on the ground."

29Then God said, "I give you every seed-bearing plant on the face of the whole earth and every tree that has fruit with seed in it. They will be yours for food. 30And to all the beasts of the earth and all the birds in the sky and all the creatures that move along the ground—everything that has the breath of life in it—I give every green plant for food." And it was so.

1. Who bears God's image?

_____

_____

_____

_____

2. What does it mean for us to bear the image of God? How might we do that in our lives today?

_____

_____

_____

_____

3. How could these verses inform the way we value other people in the world, regardless of whether they are Christians?

_____

_____

_____

_____

4. It was not God's original plan for people to rule over one another. What did God give Adam and Eve the authority to rule over?

_____

_____

_____

_____

5. What do you think "rule over" might mean in these verses? Do you think it means to dominate and ruthlessly control?

_____

_____

_____

_____

Read **Genesis 3:16–19**:

[16]*To the woman he said, "I will make your pains in childbearing very severe; with painful labor you will give birth to children. Your desire will be for your husband, and he will rule over you."*

[17]*To Adam he said, "Because you listened to your wife and ate fruit from the tree about which I commanded you, 'You must not eat from it,' cursed is the ground because of you; through painful toil you will eat food from it all the days of your life.* [18]*It will produce thorns and thistles for you, and you will eat the plants of the field.* [19]*By the sweat of your brow you will eat your food until you return to the ground, since from it you were taken; for dust you are and to dust you will return."*

When Adam and Eve sinned and were separated from God, God responded with punishment. While most Christians interpret this passage as God's disciplinary response when people separated themselves from fellowship with God, some have attempted to pull Genesis 3:16 out of its proper context and use it to prove that it was God's original will for men to rule over their wives. Notice, too, that the verse specifies "husband," not "men." No Bible verse anywhere entitles all men to rule over all women.

6. What might we conclude about the English translation "rule over" in verse 16? It's the same language used about what God expects of humanity's relationship with the rest of creation. By "rule over," do you think God expected domineering control? Why or why not?

___

___

___

___

Read **Galatians 3:26–4:7**:

[26]*So in Christ Jesus you are all children of God through faith,* [27]*for all of you who were baptized into Christ have clothed yourselves with Christ.* [28]*There is neither Jew nor Gentile, neither slave nor free, nor is there male and female, for you are all one in Christ Jesus.* [29]*If you belong to Christ, then you are Abraham's seed, and heirs according to the promise.*

¹*What I am saying is that as long as an heir is underage, he is no different from a slave, although he owns the whole estate.* ²*The heir is subject to guardians and trustees until the time set by his father.* ³*So also, when we were underage, we were in slavery under the elemental spiritual forces of the world.* ⁴*But when the set time had fully come, God sent his Son, born of a woman, born under the law,* ⁵*to redeem those under the law, that we might receive adoption to sonship.* ⁶*Because you are his sons, God sent the Spirit of his Son into our hearts, the Spirit who calls out, "Abba, Father."* ⁷*So you are no longer a slave, but God's child; and since you are his child, God has made you also an heir.*

7. When Jesus bridged the chasm of separation that we could not cross on our own, what hierarchies fell away?

   _____

   _____

   _____

   _____

8. Even though human-made structures may not recognize that hierarchical chains have been loosened, how should these verses impact the way Christ followers value others?

   _____

   _____

   _____

   _____

Read **Romans 12** and consider ways that Christ followers are expected to treat God, ourselves, and others.

Biblical Application of Lesson 5
DAY 2

In this section, we will discuss how the issue of pornography overlaps with commercial sexual exploitation. Regardless of whether pornography is an issue for you personally, this section may help shed light on the physical, psychological, and societal effects of porn use in the local community.

In light of the scriptures we have already discussed on Day 1, we can affirm that the distribution and consumption of pornography is in direct opposition with the concept of honoring people as human beings who are made in God's image. Although many Christians know that viewing pornography is a sin, they can't seem to stop. If this is your story, take heart! This section is here to encourage a change while offering a glimpse into a side of pornography that is rarely discussed or understood. It is my prayer that you find hope, encouragement, and resources to get the help you need to end your use of pornography.

Patrick Carnes, an expert on sex addiction, has dedicated his research and career to understanding the slippery slope of sex addiction and to providing tools for people to get the help they need. Carnes explains that pornography is as addictive as heroin, and he describes the process of becoming addicted to sex as similar to any other addiction. Just like chemical addiction, the consumer becomes dependent on the substance while simultaneously building up a tolerance that results in requiring more of the stimulant to achieve the same outcome. Carnes explains that an increased dependence and built-up tolerance to pornography can result in the need to view more extreme pornography in order to even become aroused—such as increased violence, fetishes, and underage pornography.[3]

Built-up tolerance can also lead to buying sex as a means of acting out a behavior the buyer may consider to be unacceptable in a committed relationship—such as

---

3. See Patrick Carnes, *Out of the Shadows: Understanding Sexual Addiction*, 3rd ed. (Center City, MN: Hazelden, 2001).

fetishes, violence, racism, sexism, and behaviors that are meant to humiliate oneself or degrade the other person.[4]

Carnes also explains that, although many sex addicts are addicted to violent or distorted forms of sex, they often appear to live normal lives in the community. Ironically, many tend to exhibit a persona of high morality and near prudishness in their regular lives. When a person in a long-term marriage who appears to be an upstanding citizen is accused of buying sex, the community often protects the perpetrator and accuses the victim of lying. Many sex addicts admit to feeling appalled by their own addiction and sincerely want to change their mindset and behavior. Carnes's work focuses on helping sex addicts identify the ways that their addiction manifests and abstain through twelve-step recovery, peer accountability, and professional counseling. His book *Out of the Shadows* is an excellent place to start.

Pornography addiction expert and author Gary Wilson dedicated his career to helping men and women recognize and overcome pornography addiction. In his book, *Your Brain on Porn*, Wilson identifies how porn addiction, like other addictions, requires increased use to achieve arousal. Wilson explains that some men who are addicted to pornography experience physical ailments such as erectile dysfunction, delayed ejaculation, or the inability to become aroused by anything except certain types of violent porn or specific fetishes. He describes how men are terrified to discuss these issues with physicians or other men, so most continue to remain isolated in their pornography addiction or act out these fetishes by paying for physical sex. Men and women who have found Wilson's book to be a helpful resource have shared their stories on Wilson's online forum.[5]

Both Patrick Carnes and Gary Wilson explain that sex addicts are often appalled by their addictions. Many have attested to initially feeling fear, shame, despair, disgust, depression, and self-harm ideation when they were isolated in their compulsive behaviors but have testified to finding hope and a way out through peer accountability, books, and resources.

---

4. See Rachel Moran, *Paid For: My Journey through Prostitution* (New York: W. W. Norton & Company, 2015).
5. See Gary Wilson, *Your Brain on Porn: Internet Pornography and the Emerging Science of Addiction* (Kent, UK: Commonwealth Publishing, 2015).

1. What do you think contributes to someone's feelings of shame around sex or pornography addiction?

_____

_____

_____

_____

_____

_____

_____

2. How could the church be a better ally for those struggling with addiction to sex and pornography instead of being a source of shame?

_____

_____

_____

_____

_____

_____

_____

_____

_____

_____

Biblical Application of Lesson 5
DAY 3

Stefanie Carnes is an author and sex addiction expert who focuses her work on helping partners of sex addicts through the process of betrayal, grief, and potential relational restoration. Her book *Mending a Shattered Heart* is an excellent resource for those who are partners or loved ones of a person struggling with pornography or other forms of sex addiction.

Jay Stringer is a Christian mental health counselor and author who focuses on sexual brokenness from a theological and therapeutic point of view. His book *Unwanted* is a powerful resource for Christians who have experienced sexual brokenness of any kind.

Refer back to the legal definition of sex trafficking found in Lesson 1 and consider the overlap between trafficking and pornography.

1. How does pornography use overlap with sex trafficking . . .
   In terms of minors?

   _____
   _____
   _____

   In terms of exchange of resources?

   _____
   _____
   _____

   In terms of force, fraud, or coercion?

   _____
   _____
   _____

If a person is forced to commit sex acts while being recorded, then anyone who watches the image or video is directly witnessing what?

_____

_____

If a person paid money to watch a coerced recorded sex act, what role did they play in the system of human trafficking?

_____

_____

2. How can the use of pornography harm . . .
The user and the user's loved ones?

_____

_____

Sex trafficking victims and survivors?

_____

_____

The user's witness as a Christ follower?

_____

_____

The user's witness as a community member?

_____

_____

Modern technology has made it easier than ever to objectify others through pornography and other forms of sexual exploitation. Pornography profits are estimated at between $6 billion and $15 billion per year in the United States alone.[6]

---

6. Ross Benes, "Porn Could Have a Bigger Economic Influence on the US than Netflix," *Yahoo! Finance*, June 20, 2018, https://www.yahoo.com/tech/porn-could-bigger-economic-influence-121524565.html?guce_referrer=.

But where technology can be used to exploit others, it can also be used to deter the purchase of online sex trafficking and hold perpetrators accountable. In a chatbot sting operation conducted by Seattle against Slavery in 2019, more than two thousand consumers tried to buy sex with a minor in a twenty-four-hour period.[7]

Since then, chatbot technology has improved and made significant progress in finding online sex buyers. Here is an excerpt from an article about how Microsoft technology, anti-trafficking nonprofits, and law enforcement have partnered to deter or arrest online sex consumers:

> In the greater Seattle area, people conduct as many as 10,000 searches for online prostitution every day, including searches to buy sex with children. Law enforcement agencies use the solution's Intercept Chatbots module to help monitor and disrupt such transactions.
>
> The law enforcement agencies use Intercept Chatbots to post decoy trafficking ads online and wait for buyers to respond. The bots—built with Language Understanding, part of Azure Cognitive Services—then use conversational AI to reply, probing prospective buyers' intentions.[8]

---

7. Washington Trafficking Prevention, "2021 TCCAT Community Conversation," February 1, 2021, https://www.youtube.com/watch?v=hufL1R29xbQ, 16:51.
8. Microsoft, "Seattle against Slavery Combats Human Trafficking and Saves Lives at Cloud Scale," Microsoft Customer Stories, September 9, 2019.

Biblical Application of Lesson 5
DAY 4

There is help! Many people who recover from substance addictions find help through community resources, support, and accountability. The same is true when you make a commitment to abstain from pornography and other forms of sex addiction. Although local communities have a long way to go to make it easier for sex addicts to get the help they need, there are many resources out there for those looking for help! Here are several ways to get started.

Books and Websites
Patrick Carnes, PhD: drpatrickcarnes.com
Gary Wilson's *Your Brain on Porn*: yourbrainonporn.com
Stefanie Carnes, PhD: https://iitap.com/page/dr_stefanie_carnes
Jay Stringer: thejourneycourse.com

Online Resources and Accountability Groups
Reboot Nation: rebootnation.org
Therapist and 12-Step Recovery Group Locator: drpatrickcarnes.com/getting-help
List of Resources for Recovering Sex Buyers: https://endsexualexploitation.org/resources

How You Can Join the Fight against Trafficking

Commercial sexual exploitation can only exist if there are people willing to view and pay for sex. One of the most effective ways to break the pattern of sex addiction is to be part of the solution.

Truck stops are high-risk areas for human trafficking, but one individual who recognized the problem and decided to lean into the existing camaraderie of long-haul truck drivers decided to make a difference. What started as a ministry initiative grew into an organization that turned long-haul truck drivers into an army of anti-trafficking allies across the United States and Canada. Find out more about **Truckers against Trafficking** at their website: truckersagainsttrafficking.org.

Many groups and organizations are making significant changes. Airports, hospitals, convenience stores, and corporations have incorporated anti-trafficking awareness and prevention into their industries in order to combat human trafficking in all its forms.

1. What industries, organizations, and groups are you part of?

   _____

   _____

   _____

2. What can you find out about the anti-trafficking work that is already being accomplished in these places you are connected to? How can you get involved with that work?

   _____

   _____

   _____

3. If no work is being done yet, what can you learn from organizations who are making a difference in other industries, and how might it be implemented in your circles of influence?

   _____

   _____

Read Paul's encouraging words in **Philippians 4:4–9** as a prayer for yourself today: *⁴Rejoice in the Lord always. I will say it again: Rejoice! ⁵Let your gentleness be evident to all. The Lord is near. ⁶Do not be anxious about anything, but in every situation, by prayer and petition, with thanksgiving, present your requests to God. ⁷And the peace of God, which transcends all understanding, will guard your hearts and your minds in Christ Jesus.*

⁸Finally, brothers and sisters, whatever is true, whatever is noble, whatever is right, whatever is pure, whatever is lovely, whatever is admirable—if anything is excellent or praiseworthy—think about such things. ⁹Whatever you have learned or received or heard from me, or seen in me—put it into practice. And the God of peace will be with you.

LESSON 6

Sexual Assault against Men and Boys

■ Organizing Principle

A Christian response recognizes male victimization and responds with compassion and dignity.

■ Learning Objectives

- Contrast the world's response with God's response to male victims of sexual assault and exploitation.
- Discover how the community has hindered men and boys in discussing sexual assault.
- Formulate strategies for church communities to be more approachable to men and boys who have suffered sexual assault.

OPENING PRAYER

Ask someone to pray briefly for the group and for this session.

FEELINGS IDENTIFICATION

Locate the Feeling Wheel at the back of the book (page 140). Take a moment to examine the wheel and identify how you are currently feeling.

When you are ready, share one or two words from the wheel that represent how you are feeling right now. Do not explain the words you chose or comment on the words that others share.

DEBRIEF THE WEEK

Share with one another what you have been processing since the last meeting, considering prior discussion and any engagement you did with the mid-week biblical application lessons. Trauma-related content can be difficult to process and discuss. This time is meant to give participants a chance to process recent content before introducing this week's topic.

LEARN TOGETHER

Statistics estimate that one (1) in six (6) men are sexual assault survivors.[1] Although it is still becoming more acceptable and common for women to share their stories publicly, our culture has provided little space for men to speak about their own traumatic experiences. If you are a man and sexual assault is part of your story, *you are not alone.*

It is important that local communities and the church offer dignity and a safe space to heal for everyone who has been traumatized. One important step in beginning to cultivate a safe space is to recognize the prevalence of sexual violence that occurs toward men and boys. Community acknowledgment paves the way for identifying the red flags of grooming and abuse, believing victims and survivors, and holding perpetrators accountable.

You may be surprised to learn that the Bible alludes to multiple men who were sexually assaulted or exploited. Most of the passages are indirect references, compared to the assault accounts of Bathsheba or Tamar, but when we study them, God's

---

1. 1 in 6, "The 1 in 6 Statistic," https://1in6.org/statistic/.

compassion toward male survivors is just as evident. Today we will focus on one man's account during the group session, and then the midweek content will go into the details of a few others.

Scripture and Discussion

Read **Acts 8:26–39** together:

²⁶Then an angel of the Lord said to Philip, "Get up and go toward the south to the road that goes down from Jerusalem to Gaza." (This is a wilderness road.) ²⁷So he got up and went. Now there was an Ethiopian eunuch, a court official of the Candace, the queen of the Ethiopians, in charge of her entire treasury. He had come to Jerusalem to worship ²⁸and was returning home; seated in his chariot, he was reading the prophet Isaiah. ²⁹Then the Spirit said to Philip, "Go over to this chariot and join it." ³⁰So Philip ran up to it and heard him reading the prophet Isaiah. He asked, "Do you understand what you are reading?" ³¹He replied, "How can I, unless someone guides me?" And he invited Philip to get in and sit beside him. ³²Now the passage of the scripture that he was reading was this:

"Like a sheep he was led to the slaughter, and like a lamb silent before its shearer, so he does not open his mouth. ³³In his humiliation justice was denied him. Who can describe his generation? For his life is taken away from the earth."

³⁴The eunuch asked Philip, "About whom, may I ask you, does the prophet say this, about himself or about someone else?" ³⁵Then Philip began to speak, and starting with this scripture he proclaimed to him the good news about Jesus. ³⁶As they were going along the road, they came to some water, and the eunuch said, "Look, here is water! What is to prevent me from being baptized?" ³⁸He commanded the chariot to stop, and both of them, Philip and the eunuch, went down into the water, and Philip baptized him. ³⁹When they came up out of the water, the Spirit of the Lord snatched Philip away; the eunuch saw him no more and went on his way rejoicing. (NRSVUE)

1. What do we learn about the man in the chariot? How is he described? (Note: Although castration—the practice of cutting off a man's testicles—was, and is, against the law of God, many ancient nations practiced it, especially with prisoners or in cases where enslaved men were assigned to guard groups of women or royalty. The

idea was to make them less threatening, less dangerous. Eunuchs are referenced elsewhere in the Bible in 2 Kings 20:16–18 and Esther 2:15).

___

2. Where did the man in the chariot come from, and what did he do for a living?

___

3. Where was the Ethiopian eunuch going, and why?

___

4. Who sent Philip to talk to the eunuch?

___

Trafficking and Discussion

Castration seems foreign to many of us in the twenty-first century, yet it is important to know that castration has been part of the shadows of history even into the present day. The United States has a dark history of slave owners inflicting castration on enslaved Black men and boys, and for similar reasons as they did in ancient times—to eliminate the perceived threat of sexual encounters with white women, to enforce a life of servitude, and as a form of punishment.[2]

After the Emancipation Proclamation, violent assaults that sometimes included castration happened to Black boys and men in the wave of lynchings that took place throughout the Jim Crow era. Castration was an extreme form of sexual violence against men and boys, but it wasn't the only way they were targeted. Slave owners also assaulted them through voyeurism, forced sexual relations, and rape.

In 2021, the United Nations reported that the number of male victims of human trafficking (both labor and sex trafficking) had increased fivefold over the past fifteen years.[3] Sexual assault and exploitation are not new to U.S. culture. Just as it existed in the shadows of legalized slavery, it still thrives in the shadows to this day. These days, surgical and chemical castration are used by multiple states as a legal punishment for sex offenders. The ethics of this practice are widely debated. Some consider it to be a proper societal response to repeat offenders while others consider the practice to be cruel and unusual.[4]

Israelite law did not allow castration, but it did unfortunately allow discrimination against the victimized. According to Deuteronomy 23:1, eunuchs were not allowed to "enter the assembly of the Lord." However, consider the following blessing that God specifically gives to eunuchs who trust in the Lord.

---

2. Yewande Adeleke, "African Male Slaves Experienced Untold Hardship during the Slave Trade Era," *Medium*, July 10, 2021, https://historyofyesterday.com/african-male-slaves-experienced-untold-hardship-during-the-slave-trade-era-b4ef68b980ed.

3. United Nations Office on Drugs and Crime, "Share of Children among Trafficking Victims Increases, Boys Five Times; COVID-19 Seen Worsening Overall Trend in Human Trafficking, Says UNODC Report," February 2, 2021, https://www.unodc.org/unodc/en/press/releases/2021/February/share-of-children-among-trafficking-victims-increases—boys-five-times-covid-19-seen-worsening-overall-trend-in-human-trafficking—says-unodc-report.html.

4. Matthew V. Daley, "A Flawed Solution to the Sex Offender Situation in the United States: The Legality of Chemical Castration for Sex Offenders," *Indiana Health Law Review* 5, no. 87 (2008): 87–122.

Read **Isaiah 56:3-8** together:

Let no foreigner who is bound to the Lord say, "The Lord will surely exclude me from his people." And let no eunuch complain, "I am only a dry tree."

⁴For this is what the Lord says:

"To the eunuchs who keep my Sabbaths, who choose what pleases me and hold fast to my covenant—⁵to them I will give within my temple and its walls a memorial and a name better than sons and daughters; I will give them an everlasting name that will endure forever. ⁶And foreigners who bind themselves to the Lord to minister to him, to love the name of the Lord, and to be his servants, all who keep the Sabbath without desecrating it and who hold fast to my covenant—⁷these I will bring to my holy mountain and give them joy in my house of prayer. Their burnt offerings and sacrifices will be accepted on my altar; for my house will be called a house of prayer for all nations."

⁸The Sovereign Lord declares—he who gathers the exiles of Israel: "I will gather still others to them besides those already gathered."

1. When a man is castrated, his ability to have descendants is taken from him. What specific blessings in the above passage do you hear for the eunuch?

_____

_____

_____

2. When Philip stood near the chariot, he saw that the Ethiopian eunuch was reading the book of Isaiah, the same book that contains God's blessing for the eunuch. Refer to **Acts 8:31–33** and read the Isaiah passage again. How might a castrated man find hope in these words?

_____

_____

_____

3. How might this passage be meaningful today for those who have been assaulted or exploited?

4. How has the church or the local community made it difficult for men and boys to talk about sexual assault?

5. How could the church community be more approachable to men and boys who are survivors of sexual assault or exploitation?

CLOSING

Throughout the Bible, God's resounding theme is to draw all to the Lord. No matter where you come from, where you have been, what you have done, or what has been done to you, God is interested in your wholeness and healing. To people who have been harmed by others, God shows comfort and dignity. To people who have harmed others, God offers conviction, repentance, and transformation.

As we each embark on our own journey of healing, God calls us to compassion for others. It is our responsibility to recognize that the community in which we live harbors sexual exploitation that thrives in the shadows, and it is our duty to do something about it.

Over these last few weeks, you have committed to yourselves and to one another to dive into the Bible and learn God's heart about trauma and our role as Christ followers to make a difference in a God-honoring way. Before we close in prayer, make a commitment to take what you have learned and get involved in your community.

1. Start with prayer: Ask the Lord to show you your community through God's eyes, and invite the Lord to commission you to participate in changes within your own circles of influence.

2. Continue to study the Bible: There are many more passages that could have been included in this curriculum. As you read the Bible, you may now notice clues of sexual assault and exploitation that perhaps you didn't before. Don't ignore those clues. Instead, notice how God responds to those situations.

3. Educate yourself on the realities of modern-day trafficking: This curriculum only scratches the surface. Read books, watch documentaries, and visit websites that have the latest anti-trafficking research. You may want to begin with the suggested resources in Appendix C.

4. Get involved: Volunteer in survivor-led or survivor-informed anti-trafficking groups and participate in trafficking prevention and awareness trainings. Work to uproot myths or biases in the community that may hinder victims from getting the help they need or shield perpetrators from consequences.

On this final week, we will close with two scriptures. Close your time together by praying these together.

Psalm 94:16–19: *Who will rise up for me against the wicked? Who will take a stand for me against evildoers? Unless the L*ORD *had given me help, I would soon have dwelt in the silence of death. When I said, "My foot is slipping," your unfailing love, L*ORD*, supported me. When anxiety was great within me, your consolation brought me joy.*

2 Corinthians 1:3–4: *Praise be to the God and Father of our Lord Jesus Christ, the Father of compassion and the God of all comfort, who comforts us in all our troubles, so that we can comfort those in any trouble with the comfort we ourselves receive from God.*

Biblical Application of Lesson 6
DAY 1

Read **2 Kings 20:16–18**:
¹⁶Then Isaiah said to Hezekiah, "Hear the word of the Lord: ¹⁷The time will surely come when everything in your palace, and all that your predecessors have stored up until this day, will be carried off to Babylon. Nothing will be left, says the Lord. ¹⁸And some of your descendants, your own flesh and blood who will be born to you, will be taken away, and they will become eunuchs in the palace of the king of Babylon."

Read **Daniel 1**:
¹In the third year of the reign of Jehoi′akim king of Judah, Nebuchadnez′zar king of Babylon came to Jerusalem and besieged it. ²And the Lord gave Jehoi′akim king of Judah into his hand, with some of the vessels of the house of God; and he brought them to the land of Shinar, to the house of his god, and placed the vessels in the treasury of his god. ³Then the king commanded Ash′penaz, his chief eunuch, to bring some of the people of Israel, both of the royal family and of the nobility, ⁴youths without blemish, handsome and skilful in all wisdom, endowed with knowledge, understanding learning, and competent to serve in the king's palace, and to teach them the letters and language of the Chalde′ans. ⁵The king assigned them a daily portion of the rich food which the king ate, and of the wine which he drank. They were to be educated for three years, and at the end of that time they were to stand before the king. ⁶Among these were Daniel, Hanani′ah, Mish′a-el, and Azari′ah of the tribe of Judah. ⁷And the chief of the eunuchs gave them names: Daniel he called Belteshaz′zar, Hanani′ah he called Shadrach, Mish′a-el he called Meshach, and Azari′ah he called Abed′nego.

⁸But Daniel resolved that he would not defile himself with the king's rich food, or with the wine which he drank; therefore he asked the chief of the eunuchs to allow him not to defile himself. ⁹And God gave Daniel favor and compassion in the sight of the chief of the eunuchs; ¹⁰and the chief of the eunuchs said to Daniel, "I fear lest my lord the king, who appointed your food and your drink, should see that you were in poorer condition than the youths who are of your own age. So you would endanger my head

with the king." ¹¹Then Daniel said to the steward whom the chief of the eunuchs had appointed over Daniel, Hanani'ah, Mish'a-el, and Azari'ah, ¹²"Test your servants for ten days; let us be given vegetables to eat and water to drink. ¹³Then let our appearance and the appearance of the youths who eat the king's rich food be observed by you, and according to what you see deal with your servants." ¹⁴So he hearkened to them in this matter, and tested them for ten days. ¹⁵At the end of ten days it was seen that they were better in appearance and fatter in flesh than all the youths who ate the king's rich food. ¹⁶So the steward took away their rich food and the wine they were to drink, and gave them vegetables.

¹⁷As for these four youths, God gave them learning and skill in all letters and wisdom; and Daniel had understanding in all visions and dreams. ¹⁸At the end of the time, when the king had commanded that they should be brought in, the chief of the eunuchs brought them in before Nebuchadnez'zar. ¹⁹And the king spoke with them, and among them all none was found like Daniel, Hanani'ah, Mish'a-el, and Azari'ah; therefore they stood before the king. ²⁰And in every matter of wisdom and understanding concerning which the king inquired of them, he found them ten times better than all the magicians and enchanters that were in all his kingdom. ²¹And Daniel continued until the first year of King Cyrus. (RSV)

1. Compare the words of Isaiah's prophecy to King Hezekiah to the situation in Daniel 1. What aspects of the prophecy seem to be definitely fulfilled in Daniel 1? What aspects are unclear?

_____

_____

_____

_____

_____

_____

_____

2. What is the supervisor's position title in verse 3 and verse 7 of Daniel 1?

3. Even though the Bible does not explicitly record that Daniel and his three friends were castrated during their time in Babylon, their supervisor is called the "chief eunuch" in verse 3 and "the chief of the eunuchs" in verse 7, implying that he is a eunuch himself and also has authority over other eunuchs in the palace. From this detail, as well as what *is* made explicit—that Daniel and his friends were enslaved in the Babylonian palace following Babylon's siege of Jerusalem and that they were given new names—how reasonable do you think it might be to infer that Daniel and his three friends would also have been castrated?[5]

---

5. The Kopelman Foundation, "DANIEL," in *Jewish Encyclopedia*, https://jewishencyclopedia.com/articles/4871-daniel.

4. List the descriptions given of Daniel and his three friends:

Daniel 1:3:

Daniel 1:4:

Daniel 1:8:

Daniel 1:15:

Daniel 1:19–20:

_____
_____
_____
_____
_____
_____

5. How did God use these men according to Daniel 1:17?

_____
_____
_____
_____
_____
_____

6. Daniel and his friends are some of the most respected biblical heroes because of their faithfulness and obedience to the Lord. How might the church interpret the miraculous works that God did through them differently if they, like the Ethiopian eunuch, were known by their victimization rather than by their faithful obedience to the Lord?

_____
_____
_____
_____
_____

Regardless of whether they would have been perceived differently, it is important to recognize that God's view of people is not based on the world's opinions. When someone is abused, what is done to them is known by God, and God will hold the perpetrator—not the victim—accountable.

7. Consider Daniel 1. Write or speak about how you would teach this passage to someone else in a way that both acknowledges the abuse of Daniel and his friends while also recognizing them as faithful leaders in the sight of God.

_____

_____

_____

_____

_____

_____

_____

_____

_____

_____

_____

_____

_____

_____

_____

_____

Biblical Application of Lesson 6
DAY 2

In Daniel 3, Hananiah, Mishael, and Azariah are now referenced only by their Babylonian names, Shadrach, Meshach, and Abednego. King Nebuchadnezzar has set them over the affairs of the province of Babylon, and they have continued to serve the king while honoring God. In Daniel 3, King Nebuchadnezzar made a golden statue in his likeness and demanded that everyone worship it. When he discovered that Shadrach, Meshach, and Abednego refused to worship his statue, the king was furious.

In their lifetime, Hananiah, Mishael, and Azariah were kidnapped, enslaved, possibly and presumably castrated, acculturated, and were now bound and facing execution by fire. The king offered them one more chance to denounce God and bow down to the statue.

Read **Daniel 3:13–18** to discover the pressure these men were under to worship the idol and to learn their response to the king:

[13]Furious with rage, Nebuchadnezzar summoned Shadrach, Meshach and Abednego. So these men were brought before the king, [14]and Nebuchadnezzar said to them, "Is it true, Shadrach, Meshach and Abednego, that you do not serve my gods or worship the image of gold I have set up? [15]Now when you hear the sound of the horn, flute, zither, lyre, harp, pipe and all kinds of music, if you are ready to fall down and worship the image I made, very good. But if you do not worship it, you will be thrown immediately into a blazing furnace. Then what god will be able to rescue you from my hand?"

[16]Shadrach, Meshach and Abednego replied to him, "King Nebuchadnezzar, we do not need to defend ourselves before you in this matter. [17]If we are thrown into the blazing furnace, the God we serve is able to deliver us from it, and he will deliver us from Your Majesty's hand. [18]But even if he does not, we want you to know, Your Majesty, that we will not serve your gods or worship the image of gold you have set up."

1. In whom did they put their faith?

   _____
   _____
   _____
   _____
   _____

2. Was their faith contingent on a certain outcome?

   _____
   _____
   _____
   _____
   _____

Read **Daniel 3:19–30**:

[19]*Then Nebuchadnezzar was furious with Shadrach, Meshach and Abednego, and his attitude toward them changed. He ordered the furnace heated seven times hotter than usual* [20]*and commanded some of the strongest soldiers in his army to tie up Shadrach, Meshach and Abednego and throw them into the blazing furnace.* [21]*So these men, wearing their robes, trousers, turbans and other clothes, were bound and thrown into the blazing furnace.* [22]*The king's command was so urgent and the furnace so hot that the flames of the fire killed the soldiers who took up Shadrach, Meshach and Abednego,* [23]*and these three men, firmly tied, fell into the blazing furnace.*

[24]*Then King Nebuchadnezzar leaped to his feet in amazement and asked his advisers, "Weren't there three men that we tied up and threw into the fire?"*

They replied, "Certainly, Your Majesty."

²⁵He said, "Look! I see four men walking around in the fire, unbound and unharmed, and the fourth looks like a son of the gods."

²⁶Nebuchadnezzar then approached the opening of the blazing furnace and shouted, "Shadrach, Meshach and Abednego, servants of the Most High God, come out! Come here!"

So Shadrach, Meshach and Abednego came out of the fire, ²⁷and the satraps, prefects, governors and royal advisers crowded around them. They saw that the fire had not harmed their bodies, nor was a hair of their heads singed; their robes were not scorched, and there was no smell of fire on them.

²⁸Then Nebuchadnezzar said, "Praise be to the God of Shadrach, Meshach and Abednego, who has sent his angel and rescued his servants! They trusted in him and defied the king's command and were willing to give up their lives rather than serve or worship any god except their own God. ²⁹Therefore I decree that the people of any nation or language who say anything against the God of Shadrach, Meshach and Abednego be cut into pieces and their houses be turned into piles of rubble, for no other god can save in this way."

³⁰Then the king promoted Shadrach, Meshach and Abednego in the province of Babylon.

3. What was the miracle that these three men experienced?

_____

_____

_____

_____

_____

_____

4. Who was the first to notice that something strange was going on in the furnace?

_____

_____

_____

_____

5. How did the king describe what he saw?

_____

_____

_____

_____

_____

_____

6. What did the king call Shadrach, Meshach, and Abednego when he called them to come out of the furnace?

_____

_____

_____

_____

_____

_____

_____

The fourth figure in the furnace is thought by some to be the first visual representation of the Messiah. If so, then Shadrach, Meshach, and Abednego were the first to walk with Jesus!

7. Rather than worshiping the idol of the Babylonian king, who began to worship the true God alongside Shadrach, Meshach, and Abednego?

_____

_____

_____

_____

_____

_____

_____

Biblical Application of Lesson 6
DAY 3

Throughout this lesson, we have focused on male trafficking and abuse survivors. Today we will look at a biblical account of a man who was labor trafficked and then became the victim of a female sexual perpetrator.

The man is Jacob and Rachel's son Joseph. Remember Rachel and Leah, the sisters who fought to have the most children? Joseph is Rachel's biological son, the youngest of all of Jacob's sons when he is born (later Benjamin is born to become the youngest), and Joseph is clearly Jacob's favorite son. As a result of Jacob's unrestrained favoritism toward Joseph, Joseph's brothers experience intense jealousy and hatred of their younger brother. In Genesis 37, Jacob sends Joseph to go find his other brothers, who are working in the field.

Read **Genesis 37:18–36**:

[18]*When Joseph's brothers saw him coming, they recognized him in the distance. As he approached, they made plans to kill him.* [19]*"Here comes the dreamer!" they said.* [20]*"Come on, let's kill him and throw him into one of these cisterns. We can tell our father, 'A wild animal has eaten him.' Then we'll see what becomes of his dreams!"*

[21]*But when Reuben heard of their scheme, he came to Joseph's rescue. "Let's not kill him," he said.* [22]*"Why should we shed any blood? Let's just throw him into this empty cistern here in the wilderness. Then he'll die without our laying a hand on him." Reuben was secretly planning to rescue Joseph and return him to his father.*

[23]*So when Joseph arrived, his brothers ripped off the beautiful robe he was wearing.* [24]*Then they grabbed him and threw him into the cistern. Now the cistern was empty; there was no water in it.* [25]*Then, just as they were sitting down to eat, they looked up and saw a caravan of camels in the distance coming toward them. It was a group of Ishmaelite traders taking a load of gum, balm, and aromatic resin from Gilead down to Egypt.*

[26]*Judah said to his brothers, "What will we gain by killing our brother? We'd have to cover up the crime.* [27]*Instead of hurting him, let's sell him to those Ishmaelite traders.*

After all, he is our brother—our own flesh and blood!" And his brothers agreed. ²⁸*So when the Ishmaelites, who were Midianite traders, came by, Joseph's brothers pulled him out of the cistern and sold him to them for twenty pieces of silver. And the traders took him to Egypt.*

²⁹*Some time later, Reuben returned to get Joseph out of the cistern. When he discovered that Joseph was missing, he tore his clothes in grief.* ³⁰*Then he went back to his brothers and lamented, "The boy is gone! What will I do now?"*

³¹*Then the brothers killed a young goat and dipped Joseph's robe in its blood.* ³²*They sent the beautiful robe to their father with this message: "Look at what we found. Doesn't this robe belong to your son?"*

³³*Their father recognized it immediately. "Yes," he said, "it is my son's robe. A wild animal must have eaten him. Joseph has clearly been torn to pieces!"* ³⁴*Then Jacob tore his clothes and dressed himself in burlap. He mourned deeply for his son for a long time.* ³⁵*His family all tried to comfort him, but he refused to be comforted. "I will go to my grave mourning for my son," he would say, and then he would weep.*

³⁶*Meanwhile, the Midianite traders arrived in Egypt, where they sold Joseph to Potiphar, an officer of Pharaoh, the king of Egypt. Potiphar was captain of the palace guard. (NLT)*

1. If this situation occurred today, it would be a textbook human-trafficking case! How might this biblical account, told in the perspective of human-trafficking awareness, work to dismantle some potential misconceptions?

_____

_____

_____

_____

_____

2. How might a parent of a trafficking survivor relate to Jacob and Rachel in this story?

_____

_____

_____

_____

_____

3. How might the church minister to family members whose loved ones have gone missing?

_____

_____

_____

_____

_____

4. How could Joseph's story—as a man of great faith and a labor-trafficking survivor—give hope to men who can relate?

_____

_____

_____

_____

_____

Read **Genesis 39:1–23**:

¹When Joseph was taken to Egypt by the Ishmaelite traders, he was purchased by Potiphar, an Egyptian officer. Potiphar was captain of the guard for Pharaoh, the king of Egypt.

²The LORD was with Joseph, so he succeeded in everything he did as he served in the home of his Egyptian master. ³Potiphar noticed this and realized that the LORD was with Joseph, giving him success in everything he did. ⁴This pleased Potiphar, so he soon made Joseph his personal attendant. He put him in charge of his entire household and everything he owned. ⁵From the day Joseph was put in charge of his master's household and property, the LORD began to bless Potiphar's household for Joseph's sake. All his household affairs ran smoothly, and his crops and livestock flourished. ⁶So Potiphar gave Joseph complete administrative responsibility over everything he owned. With Joseph there, he didn't worry about a thing—except what kind of food to eat!

Joseph was a very handsome and well-built young man, ⁷and Potiphar's wife soon began to look at him lustfully. "Come and sleep with me," she demanded.

⁸But Joseph refused. "Look," he told her, "my master trusts me with everything in his entire household. ⁹No one here has more authority than I do. He has held back nothing from me except you, because you are his wife. How could I do such a wicked thing? It would be a great sin against God."

¹⁰She kept putting pressure on Joseph day after day, but he refused to sleep with her, and he kept out of her way as much as possible. ¹¹One day, however, no one else was around when he went in to do his work. ¹²She came and grabbed him by his cloak, demanding, "Come on, sleep with me!" Joseph tore himself away, but he left his cloak in her hand as he ran from the house.

¹³When she saw that she was holding his cloak and he had fled, ¹⁴she called out to her servants. Soon all the men came running. "Look!" she said. "My husband has brought this Hebrew slave here to make fools of us! He came into my room to rape me, but I screamed. ¹⁵When he heard me scream, he ran outside and got away, but he left his cloak behind with me."

¹⁶She kept the cloak with her until her husband came home. ¹⁷Then she told him her story. "That Hebrew slave you've brought into our house tried to come in and fool

around with me," she said. ¹⁸*"But when I screamed, he ran outside, leaving his cloak with me!"*

¹⁹*Potiphar was furious when he heard his wife's story about how Joseph had treated her.* ²⁰*So he took Joseph and threw him into the prison where the king's prisoners were held, and there he remained.* ²¹*But the L*ord *was with Joseph in the prison and showed him his faithful love. And the L*ord *made Joseph a favorite with the prison warden.* ²²*Before long, the warden put Joseph in charge of all the other prisoners and over everything that happened in the prison.* ²³*The warden had no more worries, because Joseph took care of everything. The L*ord *was with him and caused everything he did to succeed.* (NLT)

5. What similarities do you see or hear between the story of Joseph and the story of Daniel, Shadrach, Meshach, and Abednego?

___

___

___

___

___

6. Although Joseph was put in authority over Potiphar's household, he was still enslaved. Who held the power in the interactions between Joseph and Potiphar's wife?

___

___

___

___

___

7. This story is often portrayed as a young man fleeing from lust. How is this interpretation dangerous to men? How is it dangerous to women?

8. How might Joseph's story as a man of great faith who survives sexual harassment and abuse give hope to men who can relate?

Biblical Application of Lesson 6
DAY 4

Congratulations! You have completed six weeks of Bible study, group discussion, and self-reflection on stories within Scripture that are not easy to discuss.

1. In the past six weeks, what scriptural account stood out to you the most and why?

   _____
   _____
   _____
   _____

2. What scripture(s) gave you hope and why?

   _____
   _____
   _____
   _____

3. How have these discussions challenged or altered your perspective on human trafficking and survivors, perpetrators, and the community?

   _____
   _____
   _____
   _____
   _____

4. What are three important concepts that you want to remember from this study?

_____

_____

_____

_____

The final group discussion concluded by encouraging you to make a commitment to take the next step in learning about CSE or by getting involved in your community. What are some practical next steps that you can make this week?

_____

_____

_____

_____

As you consider ways to get involved, read Jesus's words from **Matthew 11:27–29**:

27All things have been committed to me by my Father. No one knows the Son except the Father, and no one knows the Father except the Son and those to whom the Son chooses to reveal him.

28Come to me, all you who are weary and burdened, and I will give you rest. 29Take my yoke upon you and learn from me, for I am gentle and humble in heart, and you will find rest for your souls.

Close by writing or speaking a prayer inspired by these words of Jesus. Ask the Lord to guide you toward your next steps in anti-trafficking awareness and action. Pray for local CSE survivors, perpetrators, and your local community, and ask the Lord to help you make the commitment to challenge CSE in your life and in your circles of influence.

APPENDIX A
FEELING WHEEL

The Feeling Wheel was developed by Gloria Willcox in 1982.[1]

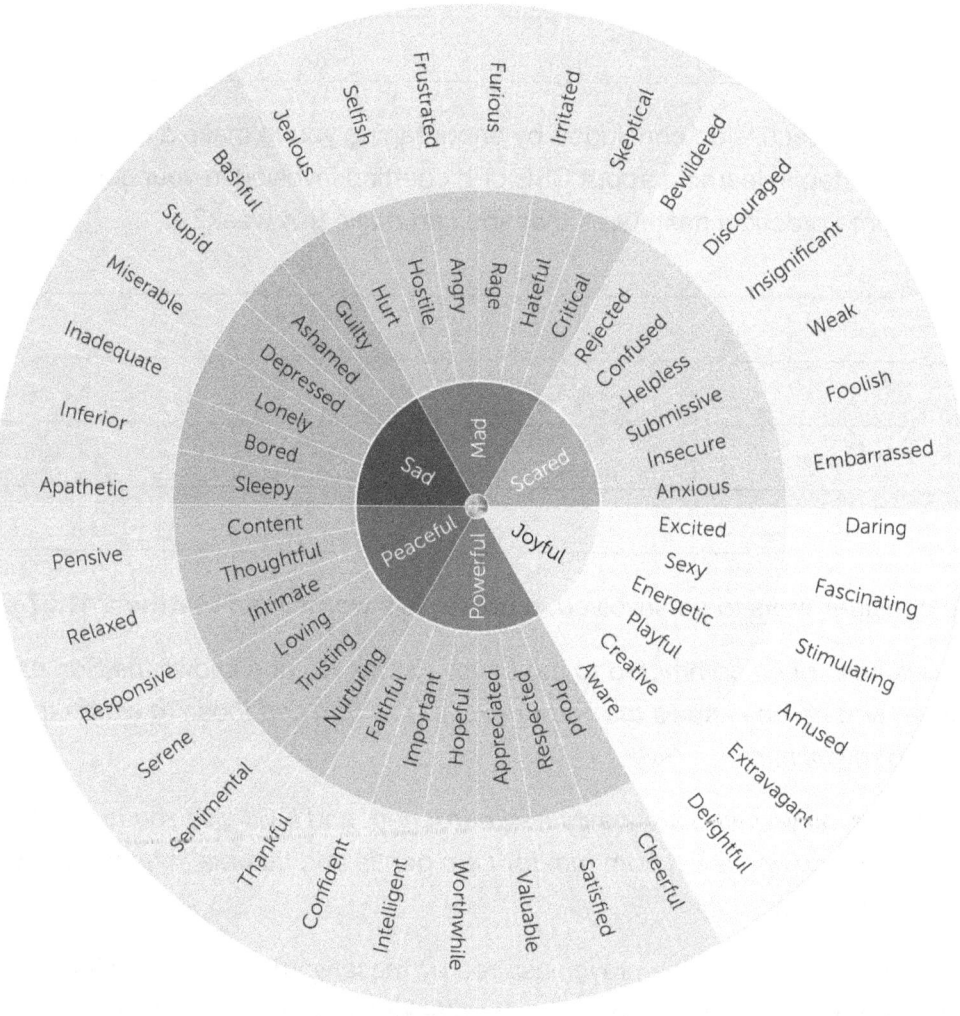

---

1. Gloria Willcox, "The Feeling Wheel," *Transactional Analysis Journal* 12, No. 4 (October 1982): 274–76, https://doi.org/10.1177/036215378201200411.

APPENDIX B
TRIGGER-REDUCING CALMING TECHNIQUES

Try these techniques whenever you are feeling stressed or triggered or otherwise deeply affected by the information in this curriculum.

1. Take a break.
Stand up and stretch. Go for a walk. Try the deep breathing or grounding techniques described below.

2. Pray.
Try debriefing your thoughts and feelings with the Lord through prayer. Pray for those who are being harmed. Pray for those who are harming others. Pray for the local community. Pray for your own openness to new information and to seeing things in a different way than you have before. Pray however you are led.

3. Practice deep breathing.
There are many great breathing techniques, but most have the following instructions in common:

- Slowly take a deep breath in through your nose. Hold for a few seconds.
- Slowly exhale through your mouth. Hold for a few seconds.
- Repeat until you are feeling calmer.
- Each breath should fill your belly rather than only filling your chest.
- The key is to find a breathing technique that works for you.

4. Practice grounding yourself.
There are many grounding techniques. This technique helps you to be grounded back in the present moment. It can be a helpful tool for those who feel overwhelmed by distressing thoughts about the past or fear of the future.

- Look at your surroundings and state what you see out loud or consciously in your head. After listing a few items, say, "And I am safe." For example: *I am sitting in my living room. I can see the fireplace, the TV, the dining room, the kitchen, the front door, and I am safe. It is seven p.m. and I am safe. I am working through some difficult material, and I am safe. I can see my dog sitting next to me on the couch, and I am safe.*

- Another option is to ground yourself by listing a few things you can see, touch, taste, smell, and hear in this moment. For example: *I can see my kitchen, my pets, my spouse, my parent, my child. I can touch my leather furniture and wooden coffee table. I can taste the coffee I had earlier or the gum I'm chewing. I can smell perfume, a scented candle, dinner cooking. I can hear birds chirping, kids playing, the cat purring, cars driving by.*

The grounding technique works well in conjunction with deep-breathing techniques.

APPENDIX C
TRAFFICKING AWARENESS RESOURCES FOR U.S. RESIDENTS

U.S. Phone Numbers
Add the following numbers to your cell phone so they are readily available:
- Human Trafficking Hotline: (888) 373-7888
- Suicide Prevention Lifeline: (800) 273-TALK
- Local Police; if there is a special number for trafficking division, add it too
- Local County Crisis Line (look it up and write it down here or put it in your phone): _____

Websites
- Human Trafficking Hotline: humantraffickinghotline.org
- National Center on Sexual Exploitation (NCSE): endsexualexploitation.org
- Polaris Project: polarisproject.org
- In Our Backyard: inourbackyard.org
- Girls Educational & Mentoring Services (GEMS): gems-girls.org
- The Lantern Project: thelantern.net
- The Journey Course through Sexual Brokenness: thejourneycourse.com

Books and Recommended Reading
- Any research articles and publications by Melissa Farley
- *Girls Like Us* by Rachel Lloyd
- *In Our Backyard* by Nita Belles
- *Mending the Shattered Heart* by Stefanie Carnes
- *Out of the Shadows* by Patrick Carnes
- *Paid For* by Rachel Moran
- *Sex Trafficking Prevention: A Trauma-Informed Approach for Parents and Professionals* by Savannah Sanders

- *The Slave Next Door* by Kevin Bales
- *Unwanted* by Jay Stringer

Trafficking Awareness and Prevention Online Trainings
- Polaris Project: polarisproject.org
- Power over Predators: poweroverpredators.org
- Truckers against Trafficking (certification offered for employees in multiple industries): truckersagainsttrafficking.org

U.S. National Hotlines
- National Suicide Prevention Lifeline: (800) 273-8255
- National Domestic Violence Hotline: (800) 799-7233
- National Sexual Assault Hotline: (800) 656-4673
- Childhelp National Child Abuse Hotline: (800) 422-4453
- Substance Abuse and Mental Health Services National Helpline: (800) 662-4357
- YouthLine: (877) 968-8491
- Rape, Abuse, and Incest National Network (RAINN) Hotline: (800) 656-4673
- National Center for Missing and Exploited Children Hotline: (800) 843-5678
- National Runaway Safeline: (800) 786-2929
- Child Find of America: (800) 426-5678

www.ingramcontent.com/pod-product-compliance
Lightning Source LLC
LaVergne TN
LVHW061252060426
835507LV00017B/2045